joy
write

Cultivating High-Impact, Low-Stakes Writing

joy
write

Ralph Fletcher

HEINEMANN
Portsmouth, NH

Heinemann
361 Hanover Street
Portsmouth, NH 03801–3912
www.heinemann.com

Offices and agents throughout the world

Figure 8.5: Emoji art supplied by http://emojione.com

Library of Congress Cataloging-in-Publication Data

Name: Fletcher, Ralph J., author.
Title: Joy write : cultivating high-impact, low-stakes writing / Ralph Fletcher.
Description: Portsmouth, NH : Heinemann, [2017]
Identifiers: LCCN 2016054764 | ISBN 9780325088808
Subjects: LCSH: English language—Composition and exercises—Study and teaching. | Children—Writing.
Classification: LCC LB1576 .F4763 2017 | DDC 372.62/3—dc23

LC record available at https://lccn.loc.gov/2016054764

ISBN: 978-0-325-08880-8

Acquisitions Editor: Holly Kim Price
Production Editor: Sean Moreau
Cover and Interior Designs: Suzanne Heiser
Typesetter: Publishers' Design and Production Services, Inc.
Manufacturing: Steve Bernier

Printed in the United States of America on acid-free paper
21 20 19 18 17 EBM 1 2 3 4 5

CONTENTS

ACKNOWLEDGMENTS

My name appears on this book as the sole author, which is deceptive because this one required a group effort. I am indebted to so many people who helped me in so many ways. My deep appreciation goes out to:

Katie Wood Ray. Katie did not edit this book, but the early dialogue I had with her helped clarify my thinking as to what territory this book might explore, and how I might approach it. I have always admired Katie as author, speaker, and now Heinemann editor. Dialoguing with someone like her stimulated me to bring my "A game."

Holly Price. Holly edited this book. I appreciate her enthusiasm for this project as well as her wise guidance. Not only that but she made an above-and-beyond effort in helping me gather necessary student samples. Thanks, Holly!

Brian Cambourne. A few years ago I had the honor of giving the Don Graves Address in Darwin, Australia. Afterward, while conducting a breakout session, I was startled to see Brian Cambourne—yes, *that* Brian Cambourne—walk into the room and take a seat. I gulped and tried not to stammer like mad. Later I got to spend some time with Brian. I found him to be disarmingly unpretentious as well as generous. His wise words enrich this book, in the same way he has enriched the entire field of literacy.

Tom Newkirk. I'm a huge fan of Tom's work—who isn't? During breakfast one morning he made a strategic suggestion that helped me untangle a knot I was having with this book. Now that's what I call a successful writing conference!

Martha Horn—friend, colleague, and legendary Christmas cookie baker—read this book in manuscript and made another pointed suggestion that helped focus the book, sharpened my thinking, and clarified what I was trying to say.

Stacey Shubitz. Stacey graciously allowed me to interview her. Plus she connected me with several teachers who made key contributions to this book.

Thanks to Dan Feigelson, Carl Anderson, Kathy Collins, and Matt Glover for conversations that stimulated my thinking. I'm grateful to have a cadre of shrewd colleagues I can bounce ideas off, and who aren't afraid to give necessary "bounce-back."

Thanks to Tom Romano.

Thanks to John Carroll, professor at the University of New Hampshire. John helped deepen my understanding of green belts in ecology, how they operate, and why they are so important.

A mega-thanks to the wise and wonderful Georgia Heard, who has been my friend for over thirty years.

A special thanks to Emily Callahan, who helped connect me to some wonderful writing samples. Emily opened my eyes to the power of backup/independent work.

Nina Bellew and I did a session on low-stakes writing at the NCTE national convention in Atlanta. It was helpful to collaborate with such a fine teacher.

Thanks to Ann Marie Corgill, Kate Norem, and Franki Sibberson.

So many other teachers assisted me with this book: Michelle Baldonado, Jody Chang, Dalila Eckstein, Debbie Goldsworthy, Sarah Grant, Julieanne Harmatz, Karen Huy, Sonja Mangrum, Beth Rogers, Margaret Simon, Tara Smith, Kathleen Sokolowski, Terry Stoufer, Carrie Tenebrini, Erika Victor, and Suzanne Whaley.

In addition I'd like to thank the following teachers: Julie Allen, Kerry Ames, Joanne Anderson, Kathleen Armstrong, Andrea Asciutto-Houck, Kari Bartels, Grant Bearden, Jennifer Bearden, Ann Beaudry-Torrey, Sherry Becker, Carla Bluhm, Dana Bolin, Ilyse Brainin, Elizabeth Brandenburg, Abby Brewer, Carrie Brotemarkle, Lisa Callis, Maria Canepa, Jennifer Carreatti, Catherine Casper, Kathryn Cazes, Terral Cesak, Amy Clark, Christy Constande, Bernita Corder, Nancy Costanzo, Shirley Cowles, Jennifer DeBortoli, Renee DeTolla, Lori DiGisi, Nina Dixon-Mauricia, Deborah Driscoll, Kristin Dunn, Marcie Ellerbie, Audrey Ellis, Steven Erb, Jennifer Erickson, Shelley Fenton, Erin Few, Gwen Flaskamp, Sharon Frost, Stephanie Fuhr, Tiffany Fuller, Sasha Gardiner-Hadford, Bernadette Garth, Valerie Golden, Mona Goodman, Jen Greene, Karen Haag, Heather Hodges, Victoria Hoehn, David Hoh, Jo Holman, Marteen Hoofer, Lisa Hughes, Leonor Jimenez-Ethier, Angela Jones, Jennie Joseph, Augustin Joshua, Michele Justus-Hobbs, Brian Kelley, Jennifer Killeen, Amy Klugman, Laura Komos, Bridget Krepcio, Maria Kruzdlo, Courtney Krzyzek, Kathryn Kuonen, Heather Lambright, Laura Larsen, Geraldine LaSala, Melissa Lawson, Melissa Leisner, Jodie Macher, Amy Makishi, Naomi Marotta, Conchetta Marucci, Kimberelle Martin, Kathleen Masone, Maura Mauck, Jen McBride, Carol McRae, Cathy Meaney, Jan Meddy, Emelie Meyer, Jessie Miller, Meghan Morden, Amanda Morrison, Lisa Mote, Holly Mueller, Adam Myman, Linda Myrick, Julie Nora, Kelly Oliver, Jodi O'Rourke, Carol Owen, Amy Painter, Megan Parker, Barbara Pastorelli, Michelle Peterson, Jennifer Petry, Leslie Popkin, Tammi Price, Beth Raff, Dolleen Ray, Robert A. Redmond, Ruth Reedy, Lynne Rerucha, Jennifer Roberts, Debbie Robi, Bree Roon, Marie Rourke, Maggie Rozell, Teri Rucinsky, Kay Scherich, Patti Schmidt, Katharine Schoeneck, Christina Schotter, Selena Seymour, Camille Shea, Jennifer Sniadecki, Susan Sokolinski, Andrea Stauch, Melissa Swanson, Julie Tersteeg, Marci Titunkik, Isabel Tuliao, Jan Turnbill, Danielle Vaccaro, Carol van

Deelen, Cathy Walker-Gilman, Suzy Wegner, Karen Wells, Diana West, Chris White, Cathy Wieland, Holly Willis, Susan Wilson, Patti Wong, Suzanne Youngblood, Juliet Zabel, and Karen Zimmerman.

I am grateful to the young writers whose work appears in this book, including Adam, Anwyn, Bolu, Brendan, Dia' Monie, Eli, Eliza, Elsa, Emily, Enrique, Erin, Hyun Su, Isaiah, Jack, Jacqueline, Jason, Jayce, Joseph, Liam, Mi Ae, Nathan, Otis, Owen, Rachel, Robbie, Sadie, Sarah, Vinny, Vannisha, and Zhao.

I appreciate my sons Taylor, Adam, Robert, and Joseph. Watching them enthusiastically produce scads of playful writing (comics, letters, stories, spoofs, and the rest) on their own time provided the foundation for this book. And I'd be remiss if I didn't mention that a new spirit in the family, my grandson Solomon, has made its way into this book.

Finally there's JoAnn Portalupi. A friend once quipped, "JoAnn has forgotten more about teaching writing than most people will ever know." She may have left the field of literacy a dozen years ago, but her influence can still be felt. JoAnn is the truest touchstone for my work, and for my heart.

INTRODUCTION: A PERSONAL NOTE

Part One of this book is titled *The Big Chill*, with apologies to the popular movie that came out in 1983. Still, you can't copyright a title, so those words are fair game. Moreover, I believe they provide an apt, if unfortunate description of today's writing classroom.

This title appealed to me for another reason. *The Big Chill* got released in 1983, which happens to be the same year I joined the Teachers College Reading and Writing Project. In the autumn of that year I started the MFA writing program at Columbia. This led to a famous first encounter, at least for me. In September I wandered uptown from 116th Street to 120th Street, walked into Teachers College, and met Lucy Calkins for the first time. She was a brand-new professor. I signed up for Lucy's first course on the teaching of writing. Soon after that I took a position with the TC Reading and Writing Project as a consultant in New York City schools, helping teachers find wiser ways of teaching writing.

I didn't realize it then, but more than taking an interesting job, I had embarked on my career. I have spent most of my professional life speaking, demonstrating, and writing books about the teaching of writing. Recently I ran into a teacher, a man in whose classroom I had worked twenty years earlier.

"Wow, you're still doing this," he marveled. "Still talking and writing about how to teach writing."

Well, yes. I believe he meant it as a compliment, though that word *still* hovered in the air. I felt a brief spasm of insecurity, and wondered if perhaps his words concealed a buried criticism. Maybe after all these years I *should* be doing something different. Many of my former colleagues have gone on to different jobs. JoAnn Portalupi, my wife and coauthor, left the field a dozen years ago and eventually became a fine artist. Me? Still talking writing, still trying to figure out the best ways to nourish young writers.

I cut my teeth on the writing process movement. I lived through its infancy, passionate youth, and mature adulthood. We grew up together. I want readers to know that this isn't a book of theoretical posturings. It's personal to me. This stuff is in my blood.

Institutional memory has been defined as a collective set of facts, concepts, experiences, and know-how held by a group of people. Because institutional memory is bigger than any one individual, it requires the ongoing transmission of these memories between members of this group. Age has always been considered something of a mixed blessing in this country ("Never trust anybody over thirty"), but after thirty-plus years in this field, well, I can't duck the fact that my years have given me a big dose of institutional memory. We certainly need strong new voices in education; Heinemann and Stenhouse have made major contributions in this regard. But it's equally important to listen to those who have been in the field long enough to have experienced the ebbs and flows, the ins and outs, the new fads and fresh expressions that eventually get replaced by newer fads and fresher expressions. Individuals with institutional memory are important to any organization. They (I) can tell you not only what things were like in the old days, but equally important—*why*.

The writing process à la Graves, Murray, Calkins, Atwell, and others was a reaction against the repressive writing practices of the 1950s and 1960s in which so many young writers felt disengaged. The writing process movement (and yes, it really was a movement) proposed a refreshing change, a bold new vision: let's allow young writers to do what real writers do.

Some professional books aim to explain and instruct. Others challenge orthodoxies and hope to prompt readers to revise their thinking. In this book I hope to do both. In Part One, I stir the pot, create discomfort with established writing dogma, and suggest better alternatives. In Part Two, I introduce a new concept: *greenbelt writing*. We'll explore writing that is low-stakes, informal, student-centered. We'll see that it is an ideal place for students to:

- find their stride as writers
- experience the joy, pleasure, and passion of writing
- define/identify themselves as writers.

In the second half of the book, we'll look at various kinds of greenbelt writing, some sparked and structured by teachers, others student-generated. I call this latter category *feral writing*, and I believe we have undervalued its importance in growing student writers.

Low-stakes writing is important because it builds muscles that strengthen other kinds of writing. But such writing is often tentative and represents a kind of thinking-on-paper. If we want to encourage it, we need to respond to it differently than we would to the traditional writing assignments.

You'll find a number of metaphors in this book. I can't help it: I'm a metaphorical thinker—maybe it's the poet in me—though I realize that people sometimes find that exasperating (just ask my wife). Still, a well-chosen metaphor does have an uncanny ability to open up a concept and lay it bare so we can grasp it.

Teachers need to rely on the very best ideas for our instruction. This involves a measure of critical thinking because not all methods are equally effective. In this book, I will describe certain prevailing approaches to teaching writing with which I don't agree. It's not my intention to bash any program, philosophy, or individual who believes in the practices put forth in such programs. However, I do think it's fair to draw distinctions between various approaches. Otherwise how can we get down to what's truly important?

In our march from womb to tomb there's only a brief time when our ideas about writing/reading are in flux: when we're forming attitudes we'll have for life. For many children, preschool is probably too early. By middle school and high school, student attitudes about writing, their identity as writers and readers, have become fixed. But during elementary school (age six to twelve), children are both intellectually aware and open-minded. Those first six grades give us rare opportunity to instill in them positive attitudes toward writing and reading. Are we taking advantage of that sweet spot, or are we squandering the opportunity?

In Plymouth, Connecticut, I ate lunch with a group of fifth-grade writers, something I often do during my author visits. While we passed around slices of pizza, I asked each boy to introduce himself as a writer. There was one boy named Jason, a kid with a soft voice that quite didn't fit with his large body.

"I like to write in my notebook," he murmured.

I nodded. "What kind of things do you write in there?"

"Well, I collect my memories there—in a good way," he said. "So I can cherish them, and have them forever."

He stated this without a shred of embarrassment. None of the other boys snickered or rolled their eyes. They understood what he was saying.

In the final analysis, my interest does not lie with policy, standards, assessments, or vying methodologies. What I care about are the kids like Jason, Emilio, Liza, Racheed, Solomon, Aaron, and Laverne. We have a few, precious years to inform their identities as writers. We must strive to see the writing curriculum through their eyes, as they experience it, from their points of view.

What kind of writers do we hope to see in our classrooms? Will they flourish or languish, be engaged or bored? Can we provide the necessary conditions so they can develop a genuine love of the craft? Having them go through the motions as we check off the various genres—is that really good enough? No, it's not. We can do better than that. I want to create the kind of writing classrooms where they can look down at the sentences they have written, and cherish every last word.

the big chill

CHAPTER 1

My Beautiful Balloon

I visited an elementary school for an author visit. After speaking to a group of fifth graders for a half hour, I asked if anybody had any questions. One boy quickly raised his hand.

"What's your bumper sticker?"

I blinked at him. "Huh?"

"Your bumper sticker," he repeated. "I mean, if you could shrink all your ideas on writing down to one thing, what would it be?"

I must confess that this question irritated me. Or maybe it was the assumption underlying this question. We live in a reductive age when complex ideas must get packaged as 140 characters for Twitter. Companies strive to streamline their missions into one easy-to-remember slogan that can be used for marketing. Nowadays branding is all the rage, a gift from the corporate world, thank you very much. Not only organizations but even people talk in these terms: "I really love his brand."

So I was dismayed to find that this branding obsession had trickled down to an elementary school. The boy's question "activated" me, as my sisters would say. I was irked by the assumption that all my ideas on writing could be condensed into one neat little sound bite. On the other hand, I could see that he wasn't trying to be a smart-ass. It was a fair question asked in good faith. I could feel the eyes of all those students gazing at me intently, awaiting my answer. I had to say *something*.

"My bumper sticker?" I repeated, stalling for time.

The boy nodded. "Yeah."

I drew a blank. C'mon, Ralph. Think! I closed my eyes and tried to concentrate. Suddenly—*bingo!*—it came to me.

"Writing is fun."

I felt the truth of those words as soon as they left my mouth. The boy nodded, apparently satisfied.

"Writing is fun," I repeated. "That's what I believe. I wouldn't do it if it wasn't."

Writing is fun. That's true for me, though I realize that not every writer would plaster that bumper sticker onto their car. Many people find writing painful. They agonize over words, phrases, sentences, and structure. They have daily battles against the monsters of self-doubt.

Writing is not all sweetness and light for me—I certainly have my struggles—but overall I consider it a pleasurable activity. A craftsperson enjoys the process of making a piece of furniture: the smell of the wood, the sound of the miter saw, the way a three-dimensional drawing gets transformed into a chair that's both functional and beautiful. In a similar way I love the "smell" of words, the crunch of sentences, the little jolt of satisfaction that comes when a strong sentence snaps cleanly into a paragraph. When I'm in my writing groove, I feel like a kid with a pile of blocks, mucking around in sentences, trying to build my city of words.

I have carried my enthusiastic attitude toward writing into my work as a teacher educator. I resonated with the writing process movement, which grew out of dissatisfaction with the prevailing scene in teaching writing. Don Murray led the revolt. Ken Macrorie was another important voice. Donald Graves took the message of writing process to the masses. After Lucy Calkins worked with Donald Graves (along with Mary Ellen Giaccobbe and Susan Sowers), she packaged writing process pedagogy into the writer's workshop—a brilliant move. Many other educators (including Nancie Atwell) would make important contributions.

The writing workshop was both elegant and stunningly simple. At its core, it still is. You gathered a group of kids, encouraged them to write about what was important to them, and turned them loose. While those children wrote, you moved around the classroom and met with them in one-to-one encounters (writing conferences). During this time, teachers listened carefully to students and, if there was time, read their writing. They enjoyed it, affirmed what they were doing well, asked a few questions, and—if the situation called for it—nudged the young writer with a suggestion or challenge. Skilled writing teachers understood that writers break easily, so they tried to use a gentle touch when doing that nudging.

The deep roots of writing process can be found in the constructivist philosophy put forth by Jean Piaget: *humans learn best through direct experience of the world.*

The writing workshop embraced this idea, devoting the bulk of its time to sustained student writing.

Minilesson: 5–10 minutes

Writing time: 25–30 minutes

Share: 10–15 minutes

But it wasn't just its elegant simplicity that made the writing workshop so remarkable. The darn thing just *worked*, day after day, even more dependably than my first Honda Accord. I experienced this hundreds of times—watching the teacher gather kids for a quick pep talk before sending them off to write. And write they did! Sure, a few kids needed extra time to get the juices flowing, but eventually even they got something onto the paper.

Writing workshop put writing on the curricular map, giving it a permanent home, a definite slot in the daily class schedule, a subject with its own sovereign importance. Educators viewed the writing workshop as a time and place for students to do the writing they wanted and needed to do. I like to envision the writing workshop (*caution: metaphor ahead*) as a hot-air balloon. For roughly an hour each day the kids and teacher would climb in and—*whoosh!*—up they'd go.

How? What forces created an upward thrust strong enough to break the binds of gravity, inertia, the daily tedium of school and lift this contraption into the sky? I would finger several important conditions:

- Kids had real *choice* in what to write about. There wasn't a lot of small print—they actually got to choose their subjects.

- This choice created *engagement*. The kids were so engrossed in their writing, the teacher and I could have an extended conversation without being interrupted.

- The kids felt a true *sense of ownership*. It wasn't the teacher's workshop—it was theirs, too.

- Students had a real *audience* for their writing, wider than the teacher. They wrote for classmates, parents, grandparents, cousins, and friends.

- There were other important *intangibles*: fun, laughter, a spirit of adventure.

- Those kids had teachers who placed a high value on *invention* and *originality* and *voice*.

There was an important reason that teachers could give students a place to experiment and take risks in their writing: we knew that we ourselves could experiment and take risks in our teaching.

So what happened? Our hot-air balloon (the writing workshop) was simple, efficient, elegant, and dependable. So, naturally, people couldn't leave it alone.

"Since you're going up anyway, maybe you could take this with you."

"What is it?"

"Preparation for the state writing test."

Uncertainly: "I don't—"

"It will take one week—two weeks, max. Then you can get back to running the workshop the way you usually do."

Uncertainly: "Well, OK."

We had our doubts and we grumbled a bit, but we added test prep to our cargo. We were relieved to see that the balloon still rose into the sky. But it didn't stop there.

"Since you're going up anyway, maybe you could spend a chunk of time focusing on persuasive writing. The Common Core is all about persuasive writing. Kids will be tested on that."

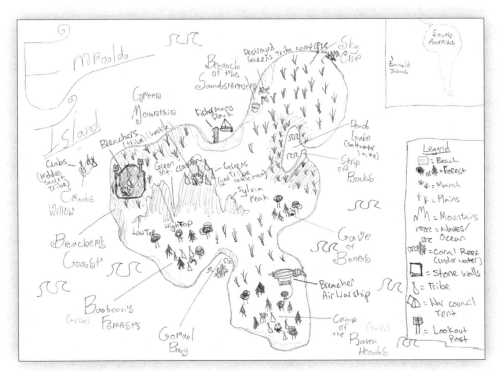

Emerald, map of imaginary island, by Jack and Eli

"But how long will that take?"

"Four or five weeks should handle it." Smile. "Piece of cake, right?"

And so we added that weighty cargo. The balloon still rose, sluggishly this time. But things felt different. Many teachers have confided to me that as more and more "stuff" got added to the writing workshop, it gradually lost its spark and sizzle.

Since you're going up anyway . . .

We went along with it. What choice did we have? But there was a definite cost. Writing was a lot less fun than it used to be. It felt a lot more like work—the not-fun kind. We finally got to the point where our beautiful balloon remained earth-stuck and no longer rose into the sky.

CHAPTER 2

Trouble in Writing Paradise

Parents know that a "swimmy" is another word for a life jacket or inflatable armband a small child might wear in a pool. In his novel *I Am Charlotte Simmons,* Tom Wolfe uses this term in regards to a high-powered college basketball team. "Swimmies" are those players whose academic excellence guarantees an overall C grade for the basketball team. This involves some bitter irony: those students never actually play in a game, but they have strong enough grades to give the team academic buoyancy and keep it afloat, grade-wise.

Let's hark back to the metaphor I used earlier: the writing workshop as a hot-air balloon. I wondered, what are the swimmies that give the workshop sufficient buoyancy so it can defy gravity and lift into the air? Even more important: what are the "sinkies" that suck the energy out of the workshop and keep it stuck on the ground? To help answer these questions I decided to survey teachers from around the country, inviting them to assess today's climate for teaching writing. I asked a number of questions.

"Think about your writing classroom over the course of the past year. When did the energy (yours as well as your students) go up? When did it go down?" Here are some responses:

- "When my energy went down, the kids' energy did as well. My energy went down when I felt like the lessons were too contrived or I was digging for something my students weren't really ready for." (Michelle Baldonado, staff developer in Los Angeles, California)

- "Energy goes up with student-directed ownership regardless if it's informational or fiction. Energy goes down when students feel compelled to jump through hoops of writing demanded of them." (Kate, fourth-grade teacher)

- "Writing energy goes up during poetry and when we walk around our building looking for places that writing hides. But in fifth grade our kids write essay after essay. The energy goes down when I say the word *essay*." (Melissa, fifth-grade teacher)

- "Simply put, not all students enjoy expository writing—they vastly prefer narrative. Incorporating a narrative nonfiction piece helps slightly, but it's like sneaking ground-up veggies into chocolate cake—it's just not as satisfying or enjoyable as the real thing." (Karen Huy, third-grade teacher)

- "Energy always goes up when the kids get to be free about what they are writing. The lack of choice stifles kids and the abundance of choice empowers kids. *Choice changes everything.*" (Anonymous; italic text mine)

I wanted to get teachers' appraisal of choice in today's writing classroom. In the survey I asked: "Do your students have more choice in reading or writing?" The results were about what I expected: 95 percent responded that their students had more choice in reading than writing.

The next question asked for a simple true or false: "My students have less choice in writing than they did five years ago"; 70 percent responded true.

I was struck by the responses to these two questions, and I think they call for some historical perspective. Back when writing process got started, students had very little choice in reading. Kids read SRA cards, or excerpts in basal readers. Today students in reading workshops enjoy the right and the privilege to choose their own books. Alas, the opposite thing has happened in the writing workshop, where choice has been severely curtailed.

I asked teachers to complete this sentence: "Compared to writing workshop five years ago, today's workshop is_____." Here's a sampling of responses:

- "More analytical and tied to text."

- "Less about student choice; more curriculum-driven."

- "More regimented, more scripted by county-supplied criteria, less teacher- and student-driven, less engaging to students."

- "Gone in most classrooms. Most teachers are teaching a specific format they believe will produce high scores. Many are only focused on writing to respond to a text."
- "Common Core Standards–driven. Focus has shifted away from exploring your own ideas. Creativity has been cast aside. Students are being directed to copy an explicit written format."

The next item on my survey said this: "The Common Core State Standards have resulted in more emphasis on expository/persuasive writing. What impact has this had on how much your students enjoy writing?"

They like it more: 8 percent.

About the same: 32 percent.

They like it less: 60 percent.

To be fair, I should acknowledge that the survey results weren't unanimous. Not all teachers viewed the climate for teaching writing in such negative terms. Some were actually upbeat and enthusiastic. Carrie Brotemarkle, a literacy coach in Reston, Virginia, said: "Compared to writing workshop five years ago, today's workshop is more engaging, explicit, and effective."

I include her comment in the spirit of candor and openness, even though it may work against my argument. No one has a monopoly on the truth. Still, I will tell you that most teachers reported being very unhappy with the way writing is being taught in today's writing workshop. Their responses struck a chord with me, not because they bolster my argument, but because they confirmed what I have observed with my own eyes.

Not long ago I visited a writing workshop in a fifth-grade class. The teacher told me ahead of time that the class had recently started a unit on persuasive writing. We met ahead of time to plan my time in her classroom. She asked me to help her students "write about big issues," which seemed like a reasonable strategy, one that all writers wrestle with. I promised to give it my best shot, and joined their workshop at 11:00 A.M. the next morning.

Fifth-grade students hold a special place in my heart. That's partly because fifth grade is the perfect age for my trade books: *Fig Pudding*, *Flying Solo*, and *Spider Boy*. But it's not just that—there is something about that middling age. When I see a group of fifth graders, with their generosity of spirit and burgeoning curiosity about the world, my heart goes out to them. I have to suppress a smile.

But these kids didn't look like happy campers. I'm pretty good at reading a classroom, and the energy in the classroom felt dead. Instead of launching into the minilesson I had planned, I decided to spend a few minutes getting to know them.

"Why don't we start by each of you telling me your name," I suggested. "And then tell me what you're writing about."

I nodded at one of the kids sitting in front.

"I'm Alison," she murmured. "I'm writing about why (garbled) are bad."

She spoke so softly that I missed the most important word.

I asked: "Did you say why *shoes* are bad?"

A few kids laughed.

Alison flushed. "Zoos!"

"Oh." I smiled and nodded at the boy sitting next to her.

"I'm Richard," he said. "I'm writing about why zoos are good."

"Francesca. I'm writing about why zoos are bad."

"Jake. Why zoos are bad."

"Ramona. Zoos are good."

These responses were uttered in a monotone, with little energy. For the first ten students the pattern held—a wall-to-wall obsession with zoos. My first, incredibly naive thought was: wow, how peculiar that all these kids want to write about the same subject! What an amazing coincidence! Perplexed, I glanced over at the teacher.

She looked chagrinned. "Uh, well, see . . . we're starting our study of persuasive writing. So for the first go-around all the kids have to write about the same issue."

I cocked a quizzical eyebrow. This didn't sound like writing workshop as I know it. "Really?"

She nodded. "Really."

It occurred to me that this new information (all the kids writing on the same topic) rendered my activity (finding out what the kids would be writing about) rather pointless. But we were halfway through the class, so we couldn't stop now. No choice but to keep going. No surprise: it turned out that the remaining kids were bullish on zoos, as well.

When we finished going around the circle the kids gazed at me expectantly. I had planned a minilesson on inserting a microstory into a persuasive essay, a strategy that still seemed applicable and highly useful to the writing these kids were engaged in. So I plowed ahead. I read aloud an example of a microstory, and suggested they consider whether a brief story like this might be an effective way to grab the reader.

The kids returned to their seats to start writing, but the energy in the room still felt subdued. It felt like these kids were laboring mightily, trying to carry heavy stones (writing about an unfamiliar topic) up a steep grade (writing in an unfamiliar genre). They were working hard, giving it their best shot. I admired that, but they didn't look like happy warriors. At one point I had a writing conference with Nathan, a boy who spoke with a heavy accent.

"Where are you from?" I asked.

"Israel."

"Ah, never been there!" I smiled. "So, what do you think about the idea of including a microstory?"

He nodded eagerly. "Yeah, I wrote one. Want to hear it?"

He read it to me, and it wasn't half bad.

"Nice job. So if you were going to put that in your writing where do you think it should go?"

He hesitated, thinking. "I don't know."

The pause lengthened. Finally he inquired: "What do you think?"

"It seems to me that you should put a great story like this right at the beginning," I suggested. "It could be your lead. That's when you really want to grab the reader, right at the start."

He nodded. "Yeah."

"What is your lead now?" I asked. "Read it to me."

"Zoos are cruel, expensive, and they make it even harder for endangered animals to survive," Nathan read. He looked up at me. "I like that sentence. I want to keep it, but I'm not sure where it should go, if I add the microstory. Should that sentence go in the first paragraph with the microstory? Like both of them together?"

I didn't want to write his essay for him. I believe it's important for kids to begin developing their own internal standards for what makes good writing. So I threw it back into his court.

"What do you think?"

He shrugged. "I don't know."

"My opinion is the sentence you wrote doesn't fit with the microstory," I told him. "They don't really go together. If it were me, I would move the sentence you wrote down to the second paragraph. That's where it seems to belong."

He nodded, picked up his pencil, and started to write. Then stopped.

"But I can't do that."

"Why not?" I asked him.

"Because that is an organizing sentence," he explained. "Mrs. _____ said the organizing sentence has to go in the first paragraph. It has to."

I smiled. "Always?"

"It has to," he insisted.

This troubled me. In the days that followed, I played and replayed this writing conference in my head. I see this not as an isolated incident but one that's indicative of the state of teaching writing. This happens all the time. Many Nathans find themselves in the same predicament.

I kept thinking about this conference. I was haunted by something Tom Romano once said me: "The two most important things in writing are *substance* (having something to say) and a *flexible use of language*."

I invited Tom to elaborate on what he meant by "a flexible use of language."

"Without a flexible, open-to-experiment, and exploratory view of language, students have less chance of achieving those surprises of meaning and language Donald Murray wrote about so well," Tom explained. "And if students are getting marked off and penalized for trying anything out of a strict norm—even if teachers think they are simply ensuring that students observe conventions—the students will become gun-shy and linguistically wary."

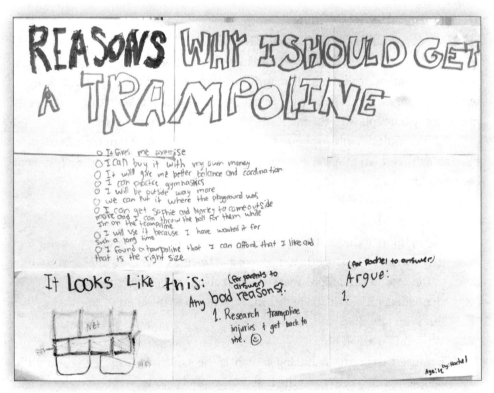

Reasons Why I Should Get a Trampoline by Rachel

Amen. Developing flexibility in young writers is crucially important because it prepares them for the myriad different writing tasks and purposes they will encounter now and in the years to come. It gives them a wider range of options they'll need to meet those challenges. Nathan was interested in expanding his repertoire of writing moves. He was intrigued by the idea of beginning his essay with an anecdote or microstory, a strategy used by many of our finest scribes, but was thwarted because he had to follow the rigid requirements of a preset formula. Where was his opportunity to use language in a flexible manner?

Perhaps it sounds like I'm being unduly harsh or hypercritical. Maybe life in today's writing classroom isn't as chilly as I'm portraying it. I only wish!

Nathan's limited options (really, he had just one) are characteristic not just of this writing program but of nearly all the programs that permeate today's writing classrooms. As we'll see in the next chapter, these programs and approaches are based on faulty assumptions about how children grow into strong, confident writers.

Limited choice, rigid structure, a preset/linear writing process, the same "teaching arc" for every genre, writing conferences that are not true dialogues but merely a chance to check up on students—all these represent "sinkies" for young writers and their teachers, killing the energy in the workshop. That's not the writing workshop as I envision it.

Some would argue that by giving young writers a definite structure and directing them to use it, such programs help students widen their repertoire and, in the long term, gain flexibility. I would counter that if students aren't invested in the writing—and empowered with the decision about whether or not to experiment with these structures and strategies—our writing balloon will not fly.

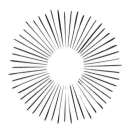

CHAPTER 3

Faulty Assumptions

To create a pearl, the oyster farmer must insert a bit of grit into each bivalve. The oyster perceives that intrusion as a threat. To protect itself, the bivalve covers it with a layer of nacreous membrane, followed by another, and another. Over time that accumulated nacre creates the iridescent pearl. In this chapter I intend to insert grit into the oyster. Or, as my dear mother would have put it, I'm going to "stir up the bees."

It seems to me that we have gotten off track. Today's writing scene is based on a handful of assumptions that are faulty. You can't erect a solid building on a cracked foundation.

Faulty Assumption # 1: A culture of compliance is preferable to a culture of engagement.

"Our district had just bought _____," one teacher told me, identifying a commercial writing program. "At our first staff meeting my principal told us to follow the program exactly as it's written. A few days later I told him I wanted to start the year having my students write poetry—not the way it's laid out in _____. My principal gave me the ol' stink eye. 'Don't cause trouble,' he warned. 'I'm serious.'"

Many teachers would tell similar stories. This principal admonished his teacher not to follow her instincts but to "get with the program," literally. He expected his staff to be compliant in this regard. And, no doubt, he felt this was a reasonable expectation, given all the money the district had spent on this program.

Compliance is trickle-down theory in action. The district adopts a writing program purportedly based on best practice instruction. Each teacher receives a kit complete with all manner of rubrics, prompts, assessments, models, lessons, videos, and other bells and whistles. A consultant flies in and provides one or several sessions of professional development, showing teachers how to use this program.

When a district is rolling out a new program, the teacher in the accompanying professional development sessions will hear the word *fidelity* repeated over and over. Fidelity means exactly what that principal told that teacher: follow the program faithfully. Listen to the experts. Don't ad-lib or second-guess.

It takes a compliant mind-set to implement any program with fidelity, without tinkering, tailoring, tweaking, skipping around, considering your perceptions of the class, or considering students' individual needs. I would argue that a compliant attitude ultimately leads to compliant/submissive students, kids who may grumble a bit but ultimately go along with our instruction about the essay or whatever academic genre is on the table.

I say: no. Stop.

Blanket compliance to any program is dangerous. Compliance doesn't allow for our intelligence, thoughtfulness, or professionalism. When we blindly comply, we hand over our ability to think and make decisions that can only be made by the teacher.

"I know many teachers who are blinded by the expectation of having students comply to pass a test," says Isabel, a fourth-grade teacher. "They've forgotten that these students are hungry for appropriate literary practices."

Choice must be curtailed, if not removed entirely, in a culture of compliance. Teachers and students who lack autonomy, who aren't encouraged to make decisions or take risks, quickly become passive and disengaged. That's not a price I'm willing to pay.

"Little of what I ask my students to write inspires even lukewarm tolerance, much less love," says Karen Huy, a third-grade teacher. "I believe it has much to do with choice, both mine and theirs. When students or teachers have real choice in writing, you start to see genuine passion."

Faulty Assumption # 2: Writing content trumps the teacher's knowledge about students.

When I work in classrooms, I talk to students about the importance of carefully reading and rereading their drafts. I tell them: "You should be the world's best expert on what you have written."

In a similar way, skilled writing teachers constantly read and reread their students' behavior—slowly and carefully building an understanding of their favorite genres, struggles, handwriting woes, breakthroughs, triumphs. They make careful note of when the energy goes up and when it goes down. This knowledge informs their teaching. The best teachers "teach at the point of their learning." Do they notice that students seem bored with essay writing? Do they need a break? This careful observation informs their instruction and reveals what students are ready to learn next. That's what formative assessment is all about.

The new world of writing instruction devalues teachers' knowledge of their students and puts a high premium on knowledge about the writing genre: craft lessons, skills, structure, and so on. Many writing programs purport to be "teacher-proof." In other words, they will work regardless of the teacher's skill. (Much has already been written about the rise of programmatic curriculum material, and the general "deskilling" of teachers, so I won't go into that here.) The result: a one-size-fits-all writing program.

In *What a Writer Needs* (2013) I argued that a skilled writing teacher draws from three distinct areas of expertise: knowledge about writing, knowledge about teaching, and knowledge about the students themselves. Certainly it's important to build students' knowledge about various writing genres. But let's remember the adage: *we teach the writer, not the writing*. We have to really know our students so we can tailor our instruction to their quirks, strengths, and areas in which they struggle. We can plant rich seeds about writing, but if we don't know our students, those seeds won't take root.

Faulty Assumption # 3: Students learn to write mainly through hands-on instruction—not by exploration and play.

A couple years ago, after a long time watching from the sidelines, I decided to roll up my pants and wade into the Twittersphere. I did because I sensed important conversations were taking place there, and wanted to be part of those discussions. Every so often I would tweet or retweet an idea that seemed relevant. One day I tweeted: "We don't teach students to write so much as create a safe space where they can teach themselves by doing."

This notion didn't seem all that profound, but it must have struck a chord because those words got retweeted more than anything else I had ever said, before or since.

Today's young writers are kept on a short leash. They don't have sufficient time and freedom to teach themselves how to write. If you take a writing class, you are likely to hear this advice: *Trust the reader.* The reader is smarter than you think. Fair enough. But isn't the same thing true in the writing classroom? We need to *trust our students*. Given the right conditions our students will grow into strong, confident writers.

I believe Piaget was right: we learn by doing, from our own experience. We learn to write by writing on a daily basis. Is it important to show students craft moves and techniques utilized by skilled writers? Of course it is. But the time we spend doing that should be counterbalanced by an equal amount of time where kids can explore, goof around, experiment, and play. (See Chapter 4.) That's how I learned to write. And I suspect most other writers would say the same thing.

Brian Cambourne, an Australian educator and author of *Conditions for Learning*, has studied classrooms that embraced two kinds of writing instruction. He calls one: "The carefully sequenced lock-step teacher-directed hierarchy of basic concepts and sub-skills approach." He calls the other: "The incidental or natural-learning approach."

Cambourne's conclusion: "The data from these classrooms suggest that when it comes to supporting the learning of writing and explaining how writers learn all its complexities, natural learning is clearly more successful."

Faulty Assumption # 4: Writing instruction should be pitched ahead of the curve—aimed at what students will need next year.

In the past few years words like *rigor* and *assessment* have dominated educational discussions. Schools have become more academic and less playful. Kindergarten teachers must teach their students thirty words, a core "academic vocabulary," not because they necessarily need them now but because they will need to know those words in first grade. I worked in one district in Illinois where second-grade teachers were trying to teach their students how to paragraph. This puzzled me.

"Most kids aren't ready to learn paragraphing until third or fourth grade," I pointed out to one teacher. "So why are we trying to teach it to second graders?"

She manufactured a sad smile. "Because they'll need to use paragraphing for a state writing test in third grade. That's why. So we teach it to them whether they are ready or not."

A language arts coordinator for a large district asked me to review the district's writing curriculum for fourth and fifth grade. The writing units on genre immersion studies were dominated by persuasion, nonfiction, and literary analysis.

"What do you think?" he asked.

I frowned. "Well, I try to imagine this curriculum from the point of view of a student. A boy. It doesn't look like a lot of fun."

"What's wrong with it?" he asked.

"Literary analysis in fourth grade?"

"Well, they're going to doing a lot of that kind of writing in middle school," he said doggedly. "We feel like we've got to prepare them."

"Pushing kids to learn something before they're ready—that can create a lot of stress," I pointed out.

"A little stress isn't such a bad thing," he countered. After more discussion we agreed to disagree.

What are they going to need next year? I would suggest that a better question is: What do they need right now? A fourth grader needs lots of free choice writing. I'd envision stretches of time where young writers could try their hands at fantasy fiction, horror, humor, comics, poetry, memoir, and multigenre nonfiction. A curriculum like that might get kids excited and inspire them to become writers.

Faulty Assumption # 5: Ownership in writing was a nice concept once upon a time, but it's irrelevant in today's more rigorous, standards-based world.

"I have insisted that children need to have ownership about their writing, to feel in control over their subjects, not to write in response to topics I give them," Donald Graves wrote. "I said this to counter decades of teaching that required children to write about the teacher's pet topics which had little to do with engaging the child" (1993).

In *Children Want to Write* (Newkirk and Kittle 2013), a book about Donald Graves, Tom Newkirk further explains the concept of ownership in writing, and why it's so important.

"Ownership was more about the relationship a student had to writing, the sense that *it was not about fulfilling a task imposed from the outside; rather it was about investing in a project that had personal meaning*," Newkirk writes. "*It was shifting from the role of student to the role of writer. It was not about a grade but about creating meaning*" (italics mine).

Today in many classrooms we find children being taught exacting writing formulas. When format dominates the writing, there's little wiggle room or opportunity for kids to make the writing their own. It may seem strident to suggest these formats are being forced on them, but let's be honest: do these students have any choice? They are directed to write in a particular genre in a way that's highly structured and externally imposed. From a student's point of view, the writing is *less about me* and *more about what the teacher tells me to do*.

Student ownership of their writing, a happy byproduct of an engagement culture, is largely missing in today's writing classroom. I'm surprised that there's so little alarm about this. But it doesn't have to be this way. Getting students engaged, making it feel like their workshop—that's the key to breathing new life into the writing workshop.

Picture Xavier. He's sitting at his desk and it's true that he's writing, but if you look closely you'll see he's just going through the motions, following a recipe that has

Scaredy Spider

Once there Was an arachnophobic Spider and his name Was Jeremy Puppy-Winkle. He was the greatest Rock climber in the web. The web Was Fly Trapper the third, located in the best Rainforest. Jeremy lived all his life until… One morning he saw a spider ands he never screamed so loud. "What a Monster!" he screamed, falling to the ground dead. Now he is an arachnophobic ghost. he roams through the Rainforest. Unfortunately he is also afraid of ghosts!!!!

Scaredy Spider by Anwyn

been handed to him. Early in the year he learned that writing is an outside game, not an inside game. Does he have any skin in this game? No. He could care less about what he's writing—mentally, he checked out twenty minutes ago. As I watch him, I'm haunted by words that Hamlet spoke when he was trying to pray but was too preoccupied to put his heart into it.

My words fly up, my thoughts remain below.

Words without thoughts never to heaven go.

CHAPTER 4

The Play Imperative

....

In play a child always behaves beyond his average age,
above his daily behavior; in play it is as though he were
a head taller than himself.
—L. S. VYGOTSKY, *MIND IN SOCIETY*

....

"Play is the work of childhood," Maria Montessori famously said. Indeed at a Montessori school you'll find a number of "work stations" set up around the room. The Montessorians refer to play as *work*. Far be it for me to second-guess the Montessorians, but I retain an enduring affection for the term *play*, which comes from the Dutch word *plein* meaning "to leap for joy, dance."

My grandson Solomon (age two and a half) often breaks into a "happy dance" when he's engrossed in play. He might set up his wooden train in a particular way, or get an action figure to perch precariously at the edge of a building. Suddenly he jumps away, churning his feet, waving his arms in delight. Moments like that bring a smile to every adult in the room. They remind us that play and pleasure are inextricably linked; you can't have one without the other. (In this chapter I will refer to Solomon, the child I know best, but I invite the reader to mentally substitute any child you know well.)

Solomon excels at playing. Nothing makes him happier than a "play bath," a misleading term because it's heavy on playing, light on bathing. Talk about stamina . . . or being in the "flow zone!" Many times I have watched Solomon play with his plastic toys for forty-five minutes, then an hour, oblivious to any adult in the room, while the bath water slowly turns tepid, then cool, and finally cold (see Figure 4.1).

It's eye opening to watch what happens when Solomon encounters a new toy or unfamiliar object. At the beginning, he seems to be thinking hard about this new thing. What is it? What category does it fall into? Blocks? Tool? Money? How might I use it? What kind of fun can I squeeze out of it?

He starts by exploring the toy, trying to get a feel for it. This exploration is not separate from or rehearsal for the play; it is part of the play itself. During this time Solomon might:

- lift it (to assess its heft and weight)

- turn it (to see all sides and angles)

Figure 4.1: Solomon having a play bath

- shake it (to see if there might be anything inside)

- taste/smell it (to see if it's edible)

- drop it (to see if it breaks)

- toss it onto the floor (to see if it rolls)

- twist and/or pull it (to see if it comes apart)

- mash it against another toy (to see if the two might connect).

JoAnn purchased a wooden bin to house old newspapers. This bin got tucked out of the way under a table, but it caught Solomon's eye. He seized it and dumped out the newspapers. He quickly figured out that the bottom part was constructed from a single piece that could be removed, so he pulled it out. He hung this bottom panel on a cabinet handle and beamed: "Look, Grandpa, I made a window!"

I remarked to my wife: "What a little devil." I was commenting on the fact that the play of children is often sly and subversive. A friend told me: "We bought our daughter a dollhouse for her birthday, but she had more fun playing with the box than the new toy!"

I showed Solomon a pair of protective earmuffs, explaining that I wear them when using my chainsaw or mowing the lawn. After watching me try them on Solomon asked if he could wear them (see Figure 4.2). They were slightly big, but I finally got them snug on his little head (producing a terrific Kodak moment). Later while rummaging through my shed, I noticed an old set of earmuffs hung on a nail. I cleaned off the cobwebs and handed them to Solomon. He broke into a quick happy dance. Then I stepped back to watch him play.

At first he was content to simply wear the earmuffs. Then he wanted to see if the muffs could detach from the metal. (They couldn't.) After that he wanted to see if he could lift out the rubber foam in the earpiece. (He could, but I told him not to.) Next he brought the earmuffs to a go-cart that my brother-in-law had loaned us. The earmuffs were springy, so he clamped them over the piece of wood in front, creating a makeshift steering wheel.

And still he wasn't finished. A half hour later he discovered that the springy earmuffs would fit around his waist, with the muffs located at his hips. Tool belt! I dug up a few extra screwdrivers plus my weed-puller, and before long our minimechanic was equipped to fix just about anything. Solomon knew exactly what those protective earmuffs were for, but when he played with them he didn't confine himself to that "assigned use." He gave himself wide latitude to use that object in all kinds of ways.

Figure 4.2: Solomon with protective earmuffs

Solomon's play includes lots of pretending. This requires a make-believe attitude and suspension of disbelief. One evening I watched him guide two plastic boats through the bath when suddenly his voice rose in mock alarm.

"The red boat has a leak on the bottom!" His eyes grew wide. "The red boat can't float anymore, Grandpa. It's gonna sink! And there's lots of *sharks* in the water!"

I joined in the game. "Oh no! Can anybody help?"

"The blue boat can help it!" he cried. Sure enough, Blue Boat steamed in to make a heroic rescue.

OK—this discussion about play is fun, but does it have anything to do with writing? I would argue that it absolutely does.

Writers play. They do so in ways that are quite similar to the play in which Solomon is engaged. This kind of writerly play starts with a period of prolonged exploration. A writer with a new idea might:

- turn the idea over in her mind (to see all the angles)

- shake it (to see if there could be something inside: a back story, striking anecdote, historical significance, and so on)

- twist it (to see if might be broken into smaller, more manageable chunks or parts)

- connect it to another subject or idea.

It's worth noting that writerly play, too, is often sly and subversive. Writers take great pride and pleasure in not following the rules. We expect them to be edgy, so much so that we are disappointed when they meekly follow the pack and produce conventional writing.

Writerly play, too, involves pretending. Pretending is a prolonged simulation lubricated by a generous dollop of imagination. That's exactly what Rick Bragg (2002) does at the beginning of an article he wrote about the Olympic sport of skeleton:

> Picture riding the lid of a turkey roaster pan down a roller coaster rail after an ice storm. Picture it at almost 80 miles an hour, with wicked turns, at G-forces so powerful that you cannot raise your helmet from the ice, which glitters just an inch away.

What is it like to ride a skeleton sled down a steep icy chute? To conjure up this experience, Bragg asks the reader to pretend, to put yourself into the scene, to imagine experiencing this suicidal ride. Writers of every genre utilize this strategy.

Recently I read several articles about the octopus as escape artist. Some accounts read like they've been excerpted from *Ripley's Believe It or Not!* One determined octopus in New Zealand somehow climbed out of its tank, clambered down to the floor, flopped its way across a dry hallway, crawled up to another tank, squeezed in, devoured a fish or lobster, and then, with its belly full, made the reverse trip back to its tank. These articles sparked my imagination. I started thinking: perhaps I should try to write about these intelligent creatures. But how? During my initial musing, I asked myself: What is it? What could it be? What category would it fall into? What form could it take? What might be the best genre(s) for approaching this subject? A straight nonfiction feature article? Picture book? Chapter book? Playful essay? Collection of poems? Mock interview with the octopus itself? A story? Would it work best to tell it from my own perspective, or that of a naturalist, or perhaps from the octopus's point of view? How might it be read? What would be my ultimate purpose? To entertain? Make people laugh? Inform? Persuade restaurants to stop including octopus and calamari on their menu? Or perhaps a combination of several of these?

This kind of loose, playful thinking (What if . . . ? Could I . . . ? Might this work as a . . . ?) is essential for all writers in all kinds of writing. A writer needs wide latitude so she can bring all her intelligence and imagination to the task. It goes without saying that assigning a particular format—a hamburger essay, for instance—will torpedo the writer's ability to play. It would be akin to telling a chef: "Make me a delicious dinner but don't use any spices, or salt, or butter." It would be like giving Solomon a box in which my new computer arrived and instructing him: "You can have the box, but just remember that it can't be a fort, a trap, a castle, a car repair garage, a Dunkin' Donuts coffeehouse, Grandpa and Noni's house, or a swimming pool. It must be a computer box, and it has to be used in that particular way."

Solomon brings certain attitudes to this kind of intense play, ones that are helpful to any writer:

- Abundant time. There's no need to rush. This thingamajig will reveal itself in good time.

- Open heart and flexible thinking. If it can't be made to work in one manner, try another way.

- Sly/mischievous/subversive thinking. This is useful because the most surprising or unexpected approach often turns out to be best.

- An expectation of pleasure. I'm going to have fun writing about this, just as Solomon knows he's going to have fun playing with it.

- Everything is potentially interesting. Little kids know that just about anything can be fun to play with: a stick, rock, Styrofoam packing peanuts, bubble wrap, the transparent plastic sleeve used to house a car registration. That assumption drives writers as well. John McPhee (1967) wrote an entire book about the orange. Given the right conditions with sufficient latitude, and a healthy dollop of playfulness, a skilled writer can make just about any subject come alive.

Play in writing is not just a nice idea—it's essential. Often it's the ingredient that closes the deal with the reader. But when it comes to playful writing, the current writing scene (dominated by programmatic instruction, with a heavy reliance on rubrics, anchor texts, and Common Core State Standards) is a gigantic buzz kill. Playful writing samples have become almost extinct. Fortunately, the news on this front is not all bleak. There is one writing realm where play shows no sign of disappearing. In fact, it's stronger than ever.

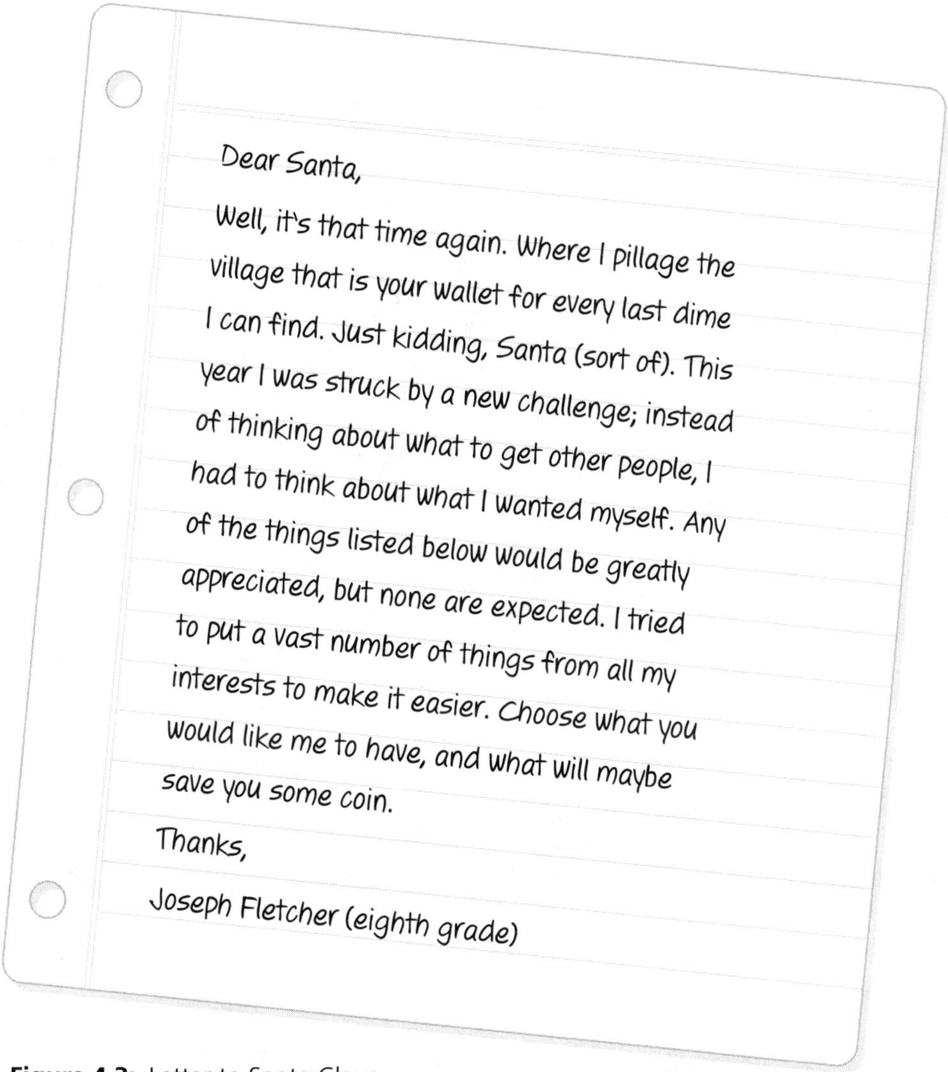

Dear Santa,

Well, it's that time again. Where I pillage the village that is your wallet for every last dime I can find. Just kidding, Santa (sort of). This year I was struck by a new challenge; instead of thinking about what to get other people, I had to think about what I wanted myself. Any of the things listed below would be greatly appreciated, but none are expected. I tried to put a vast number of things from all my interests to make it easier. Choose what you would like me to have, and what will maybe save you some coin.

Thanks,

Joseph Fletcher (eighth grade)

Figure 4.3: Letter to Santa Claus

My Mom's Jiggly Tummy by Sarah

My mommy's tummy is like a Pilow. It is even softer.

When I lay on my mommy's tummy it jiggls.

She has love handls. I notis them evry night.

I love my mommy!

a writing greenbelt

CHAPTER 5

Greenbelt Writing

His food in a can is tame and mild, so he's gone out for
something wild.

—LOIS EHLERT, *FEATHERS FOR LUNCH*

In recent years the writing workshop has become more restrictive. It is less free-flowing, less student-centered, with less value placed on the creative part of creative writing. Academic genres, fueled by the standards movement, now proliferate. The workshop has become more content-rich and rigorous. From a kid's point of view, writing is much harder. This may not sound like such a bad thing, at least at first blush, though many teachers have observed an alarming trend—diminished energy, excitement, and investment from their young writers.

The purist in me wants to offer this advice: forget all those academic genres. Or, at the very least, cut them way back. Close your classroom door and design a writing curriculum that makes sense for your students. Some teachers have done exactly that (#subterraneanteaching), but if you're an untenured teacher, just trying to hang on to your job, this option may not seem feasible. Many teachers find themselves trapped between a rock (rigid curriculum) and a hard place (students who no longer love writing).

What to do?

The problem seems intractable, but I believe there is a solution. To find it, let's turn to a completely different realm, the world of community planning and land management. Stay with me, reader. You have already watched me insert grit into bivalves, and accompanied me on a hot-air balloon ride, but I think we'll find that the metaphor in this chapter is the one that offers the most hope.

The U.S. population has grown steadily since the first census in 1790. Although the rate of increase has slowed, the total population continues to increase. In 1940 there were roughly 142 million Americans living in this country. By 2000 that number had more than doubled to 291 million. Today there are about 320 million people living in this country. A growing population creates a demand for roads, power lines, and affordable housing, and puts tremendous pressure on our natural resources. This is an undeniable impact of population growth: wooded land gets subdivided, cleared, and developed to build houses. This creates a host of new problems including pollution and erosion, not to mention the loss of habitat for wildlife.

Recognizing the dangers of unchecked growth and urban sprawl, many community planners have embraced the idea of a greenbelt. This is not a new concept (the idea actually got mentioned in the Old Testament), though it has been refined in modern times. A greenbelt—sometimes called a green way or green wedge—is an invisible line designating a border around a certain area, preventing development of that area, and allowing wildlife to return and be established. The objectives of greenbelt policy include:

- protecting natural environments
- improving air quality within urban areas
- ensuring that urban dwellers have access to countryside
- protecting the unique character of rural communities.

"It's all about connectivity," says John Carroll, professor of Natural Resources at the University of New Hampshire. "Greenbelts create a passageway allowing species to move from one habitat to another. That's critically important for the survival of those species."

Carroll explained to me the ecological value of a greenbelt, but emphasized the value to communities as well: cleaner air and water, plus enhanced outdoor recreation opportunities (camping, biking, boating) close to cities and towns.

"And there's a psychological value, too," he points out. "There's a comfort just knowing that wildland is there, whether or not you actually use it."

It is a fundamental axiom of ecology that *diversity leads to stability*. When you start limiting diversity—a manicured lawn, for example, that contains a single kind of grass—the ecosystem quickly gets unstable and vulnerable. With its wider diversity, a greenbelt brings a measure of ecological stability into a developed area.

Some wildlife can thrive without a greenbelt. Robins, sparrows, crows, rabbits, voles, and skunks can survive perfectly well within the confines of a neighborhood development. But many other species of birds, mammals, reptiles, fish, plants, and trees need the conditions provided by raw, wild forest. Otherwise they will struggle and eventually disappear.

All well and good. But what does all this have to do with teaching writing?

In recent years the writing workshop has come under intense pressure: state writing tests, Common Core State Standards, various commercial programs. Writing workshop as we once knew it has been "developed." Many old-growth trees have been cut down. A great deal of curricular land has been cleared, parceled off, and subdivided. It's harder and harder to find the essential wildness—the unique intelligence found whenever children freely express themselves—that once infused the workshop.

In this book I'm proposing a new concept: *greenbelt writing*.

Writing that is raw, unmanicured, uncurated.

I'm talking about informal writing. Writing that is wild, like the pungent skunk cabbage that sprouts haphazardly along the edge of a swamp.

I'm talking about low-stakes writing, the kind of comfortable composing kids do when they know there's no one looking over their shoulder.

Some educators would insist that writing workshop must continue in its more developed, academic form. "The reality of schools . . ." I don't agree—but that's a battle for another day. If, for argument sake, I do concede this, I would add that it's essential to supplement it with a greenbelt, a wild territory where kids can rediscover the power of writing that is:

- personal
- passionate
- joyful
- whimsical
- playful
- infused with choice, humor, and voice
- reflective of the quirkiness of childhood.

It's true that some kids, like some species, may be able to survive and even thrive in this more developed workshop atmosphere. But I submit that many students find today's writing workshop too narrow and constricting for them to generate any enthusiasm for writing. Those writers would benefit from being allowed to do more writing that is free and unguided—writing that they generate themselves.

Would those kids still participate in the writing workshop? Certainly. But I believe we'll find that their greenbelt writing will spark them, engage their imaginations, and help them find their stride as writers.

Simply put: let's make sure that kids have spaces and opportunities to experience the pleasure of writing.

What do kids remember about their teachers? Passion, a sense of humor, making things fun, and genuine caring—a sense that each student matters.

What will kids remember about writing in school? I want them to remember similar things—writing that is fun, passionate, and joyful, and reflects what matters to each student. This is the best way I know to create writing classrooms where the student can develop the concept: *I am a writer*.

In the next few chapters we'll look at various examples of greenbelt writing. This concept raises questions, among them being: how should we as teachers respond to this kind of writing? Or should we respond at all? Is this a teacher-free zone?

No.

The operative phrase for a natural greenbelt is not *keep out* but *hands off*. We might decide to walk through an area like this to savor the quiet, maybe to sample a few wild blackberries growing there. But nobody ever visits a greenbelt hoping to improve it by pruning, weeding, clearing brush, and so on. These areas are, by design,

Comics by Otis

unmanicured. Officials might opt to protect its borders by posting a sign, or erect a small fence to keep litter from blowing in, but that's about it. Once a corridor of land has been designated as a greenbelt, we leave it alone.

A greenbelt doesn't have to be managed. Indeed, its very wildness is its virtue. The same principal holds true for greenbelt writing. We need to recognize its value, establish its sovereignty, and then get out of the way—leave it alone.

CHAPTER 6

The Slice of Life Challenge

The Slice of Life Challenge is the brainchild of Stacey Shubitz, founding member of the influential *Two Writing Teachers* blog. She is also coauthor of *Day by Day: Refining Writing Workshop Through 180 Days of Reflective Practice* (Ayers and Shubitz 2010). In February 2008 Stacey was reading one of her fourth grader's writer's notebooks, and came across a piece of writing about his sister's lost necklace.

"Christian wrote an entry about the outrage he felt when his mother made the family drop everything to search for his sister's lost necklace in their apartment," Stacey recalls. "Thirty minutes after they lifted up couch cushions and checked under all of the beds, her necklace turned up . . . on her neck! This little snippet of Christian's life awakened something in me. It reminded me of 'slice of life' stories I had seen on the CBS-NY News when I was living in Manhattan in my early twenties. I realized Christian had written a slice of life entry. I thought it might be a good idea to inspire some of my other students to write with more gusto (since not all of them were writing with the regularity and interest that Christian was)."

With Christian's permission Stacey showed his piece to her class. Then she challenged her students to write one slice of life story in their writer's notebook daily for the entire month of March. Why that particular month? Stacey had lost her grandmother in March of the previous year and thought that involving her students in such writing might be a welcome distraction to keep from feeling sad about her passing. Her students rose to the challenge. Four out of twenty students created a slice of life entry every day of the month; eight students "sliced" for twenty-five of the thirty-one days. Student participation was even higher the following year.

The Slice of Life Challenge has grown each year since then. Adults, classroom teachers, and their students across six continents participate in this weekly challenge as well as in the monthlong challenge in March. Today students from all over the United States and around the world, from first grade to high school, participate in the Slice of Life Challenge. Often a class will partner with another class, allowing kids to comment on each other's writing. (The logistics can be found on the *Two Writing Teachers* blog: https://twowritingteachers.org/challenges/.) The monthlong Classroom Slice of Life Challenge was launched in 2013 as a response to requests from teachers who wanted to fuel their students' writing with a Slice of Life Story Challenge experience of their own.

"All teachers who take part in the Classroom Slice of Life Story Challenge must participate in our individual/adult challenge," Stacey Shubitz says.

The teachers I interviewed were enthusiastic about Slice of Life (the common acronym is SOL). Erika Victor teaches fourth grade at the International School of Kuala Lumpur in Malaysia. She presented the Slice of Life Classroom Challenge to her students, inviting them to write in a blog or notebook for as long as they wished. (Note: Although most teachers use a blog for the Slice of Life Challenge, some use notebooks because of consent and safety issues involved with maintaining a blog.) Erika was impressed both with the quantity and the quality of her students' writing.

"So many of them showed their inner selves and were inspired by other writers in this forum as well," Erika says. "A former student of mine made it a point to comment on as many of their posts as possible because she recalled growing as a writer as a result of this month."

Margaret Simon, a teacher in New Iberia, Louisiana, has been involved with the Slice of Life Challenge for the past five years.

"We started by creating a chart together of possible topics for slices," she says. "I shared one or two of my own slices. Their main audience is their classmates, but because I teach at two different schools, my students have a wider audience. We also connect with other Kidblog classes."

Margaret said the Slice of Life Challenge created a spark with her students, one that extended even after the challenge ended.

"Just today one of my kids said: 'I want to write a Slice of Life piece about the rat in the cafeteria,'" Margaret told me. "So my students are still seeing things as possible slices, even after it's over."

I asked Margaret what stands out to her about her students' Slice of Life posts.

"Voice," she replied without hesitation. "When my students write informally they are much more likely to use their own voice. And as the students write these life slices their writing gains fluency as well."

"Why is voice important?" I asked.

"A strong voice helps draw the interest of your reader," Margaret replied. "Voice gives confidence to the reader. And voice involves higher-level thinking skills in the student writer."

(This is a Slice of Life post from one of Margaret Simon's students. Emily, a fifth grader who was nominated as "student of the year," decided to write about her interview failure. The strong voice in this piece is backed by an unflinching honesty.)

> On the 21st I had an interview for student of the year for the parish. Let me tell you it was really scary. I was really nervous. But my cousin Nikki that brought me there told me to be brave and that I could do it.
>
> I made the worst mistake ever. They asked me if anyone has ever called me brave. And guess what my little self said . . . I said NO. I know you are all like: Emily how dumb can you be? I know it was a dumb mistake, but i panicked and just said an answer. I'm saying it now. I'm sorry my fellow Caneview Students. And while I'm on the roll of all the dumb thing that i did . . . when they asked me the most important question I couldn't answer, the words just did not come out. Then they asked one of those questions where Oh, you-don't-know-what- to-say-I-will-help-you-out-so-you-don't-look-dumb-in-front-of-everybody type of question.
>
> My dad got a letter saying that I didn't get it for the district. i am disappointed in myself. But, I did my best and that's all that I can do. Hopefully in 8th or 12th grade. I promise that I will do much better and be more prepared. I guess that bringing my lucky Grumpy Cat didn't really work. I know that people are still proud of me anyway. So, this is my sincere apology to my school members for letting you down.

As I interviewed these teachers, and read the SOL posts, I found myself wondering whether slice of life writing should be considered greenbelt/informal writing. True, the writing takes place outside the traditional writing workshop, but it doesn't feel completely wild. For one thing, a teacher must initiate and monitor it. And topic choice is partially limited in that students write about realistic events that happen during their daily life. I asked several teachers about this.

"I consider it informal writing," said Beth Rogers, a fifth-grade teacher in Clarkston, Michigan. "There is not the same process of drafting, revising, and editing as there is when my students are working through our writing program."

What makes the Slice of Life Challenge so successful? It would seem to embrace many of the conditions that allow young writers to thrive:

- The writing is personal.
- It involves frequent, friendly feedback.
- It de-emphasizes mechanics.

"My rule of thumb was that your writing needs to be understood by others, so it was important for all children to do their best writing when drafting their slice of life story," Stacey Shubitz explains. "Most teachers de-emphasize GUMS (grammar, usage, mechanics, and spelling) for the Slice of Life Challenge because it's about building writing stamina and enhancing the classroom community of writers."

Audience and expectation are crucial factors in all greenbelt writing. Indeed, audience plays a big role here. Students as well as their teachers involved with the Slice of Life Challenge know that they will instantly find readers, some from other parts of the world, who are keenly interested in what they have written.

"My students know they are writing for a larger audience, and that makes it real for them in ways that other classroom writing is not," Beth Rogers says.

I interviewed Vannisha, a sixth-grade student in Louisiana. I asked if she thought participating in this challenge has made her a better writer.

"Yes, because it helps me learn how to write about stories and think about an audience," Vannisha said. "When I'm writing an SOL piece, I think my audience is other classmates, which means that my writing should be more casual and normal."

"I love that I can use this writing to share my feelings," said Erin, a fourth-grade student from the same district. "It has made me a better writer because it helped me to start talking about my feelings and not just hide them away. When I write about slices of life, I think about my family because we struggle with a lot of things and I want [readers] to know how I feel."

Many teachers have noticed more enthusiastic writers when their students participated in the Slice of Life Challenge.

"This was the first year my class participated in the Slice of Life Challenge for March," says Kathleen Sokolowski, a third-grade teacher. "I never gave students any topics, and I made the challenge optional. Many of my students really embraced the idea. They blogged in the evenings, weekends, and after school hours. This showed me that they really owned the writing."

I want to highlight Kathleen's decision to make the Slice of Life Challenge optional for her students. Those kids had to decide whether or not they wanted to participate, which is crucial.

"The Slice of Life Challenge addresses several needs," said Stacey Shubitz. "First, it is informal, low-stakes writing. It is ungraded. If anyone is grading it, well, they're doing it wrong! Second, it is meant to increase students' writing stamina by having them write frequently. Third, it's about *their life*. There are no assigned topics or prompts, which allows kids flexibility and freedom with their topic choices. Fourth, it's about living a wide-awake life, looking for small moments that are worthy of capturing. Finally, it is meant to challenge kids to live like a writer for an entire month. This isn't easy work. However, the impact can be huge."

Other teachers agree. Dalila Eckstein, a third-grade teacher in Gladwyne, Pennsylvania, has seen the benefits of the Slice of Life Challenge spill into other forms of writing, as well.

"Slice of life writing—really any type of nonrequired writing—is what allows students to develop their own writing identities," Dalila says. "I have found that I can capitalize on these other types of writing when providing instruction in more structured, 'required' types of writing. This year, in particular, as I taught my students to write in various structured ways, I found myself constantly calling out writer moves they had made in their more informal writing."

I suspect one important reason the Slice of Life Challenge has caught on is that it feels like a refreshing antidote to the more prescriptive writing found in so many writing classrooms.

"My students enjoy the Slice of Life Challenge and the freedom it brings to an otherwise very structured writing time," Beth Rogers told me. "I have been trying to build in more freedom to allow students to engage in purposeful, meaningful writing and reading. They crave it, and when they have that freedom, they fly."

Slice of Life Posts from Students

A Rainy Day (by Jacqueline, Fifth-Grade Student in Beth Rogers' Class)

"Ugh! I'm soooo bored!" my youngest sister, Amelia whined. "It's too wet outside to do anything fun!" she drooped over like a plant that hadn't been watered in weeks. Six is a tough age. The soft pitter patter of the rain made me shiver. She was right . . . there really was nothing to do.

"That's silly." I replied, trying to seem upbeat. She looked at me with a puzzled expression on her face. "I didn't tell a joke," she pointed out, not getting what I was saying. I smiled and moved on. "We can do tons of fun things inside!" I giggled when she looked at me again, her eyes looking very suspicious. "What kinds of things?" she asked, finally standing up. "Well," I started, but then stopped quickly. I hadn't really thought about what we could do. "Um, we could build . . . I mean, we might be able to . . ." I struggled to think but I had to at least try. Who could refuse those eyes?

"I know what your saying! We could build a fort! Or a clubhouse. You could teach me how to read in it! Thanks Jacqueline!" With that she bolted up the stairs, leaving me dumbfounded. I guessed I would have to build the fort, since she probably didn't know how to. I ran up the stairs after her and panted while I walked to her room.

To my surprise she had a plan and soon Fort Reading was made. Thunder crashed and rain pounded the windows, making the whole house seem like it was alive and dancing, but I really didn't care. I was teaching one of my favorite people how to do my favorite thing. I was reading with Amelia!

Mike and Ike Fight (by Adam, Fifth-Grade Student in Beth Rogers' Class)

"Can we have those Mike and Ike's?" I asked Will. Blake and I were at Will's house and were having a sleepover. "Sure, just don't spill them," he replied. Blake and I ran to the table and grabbed the Mike and Ike's. We tore the box open and ran back to the couch.

We were eating them so fast there was only 10 left. I took out two and ate them. Then Blake took the box, and ate two. There was six left. By now we were all fighting for them. Blake and I were tugging on the box until Will took the box. He dumped the box in his mouth but two fell. Will got on the ground and picked them up. He threw one, but I didn't know where.

"Mouth me!" I yelled as I opened my mouth. Will threw the last one and it plopped right in my mouth.

"Haha," I said to Blake.

Just as we sat back on the couch, we turned on the TV. I started to laugh because I was thinking: why we were fighting over candy.

Note to Mom from Elsa

CHAPTER 7

A Classroom Notebook

Emily Callahan teaches fifth grade in Kansas City. She has a passion for teaching writing. Emily told me: "The idea of giving kids time, choice, and multiple opportunities to show their thinking in whatever ways work for them is a driving force in my room."

One autumn day a former student came to visit her class. They were chatting when the girl suddenly blurted, "I think you should have a class writer's notebook."

Emily paused. In past years each of her students had kept individual writer's notebooks, but she had never considered the idea of a collective writer's notebook for the class. The idea intrigued her.

"OK, yes," she said. "Let's do this!"

A student in her class overheard this conversation. "There's a cool blue notebook on your back counter—can we use that?"

"Go for it," Emily encouraged him.

He grabbed the notebook and took it home. That night he wrote a poem on the first page about being the first one to write in the class notebook. Other kids wanted to write in it, and the notebook circulated around the room. One week Robbie wrote about a new LEGO® set. Mercy wrote about needing God in her life. Jake wrote about his enduring love for chocolate. Other kids chose to write poems or little memory tidbits. In many cases they were inspired by entries written by their peers (see Figure 7.1).

"Sometimes they don't write their own entries but give each other feedback, ask questions to the writer," Emily says. "Spelling and grammar isn't the focus."

I tend to envision the writer's notebook as a solitary endeavor, but the success of Emily's class notebook has made me rethink this notion. Indeed, I'm intrigued by the way entries written by one student may "rub off" and inspire another.

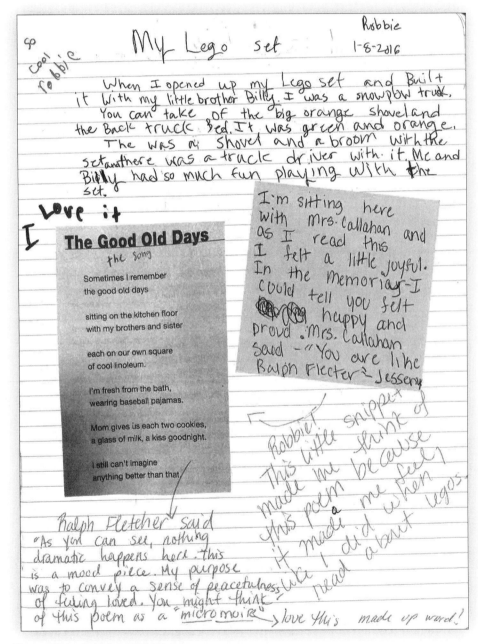

Figure 7.1: Robbie's LEGO® set

The responses from a survey about the class writer's notebook (see Figure 7.2) indicated that finding an audience and not feeling pressured by time were important conditions. The classroom notebook is not the only example of informal, low-stakes writing that takes place in Emily's classroom. Indeed, her whole classroom is a writing greenbelt. I'll outline a variety of writing greenbelt opportunities for students below.

Wonder Notebooks

This idea was inspired by Georgia Heard, coauthor of *A Place for Wonder: Reading and Writing Nonfiction in the Primary Grades* (Heard and McDonough 2009).

"Nurturing children's natural sense of wonder fosters a love of learning, creativity, and an insatiable curiosity in and outside of the classroom," Georgia says. "Teachers need to protect and care for this sense of

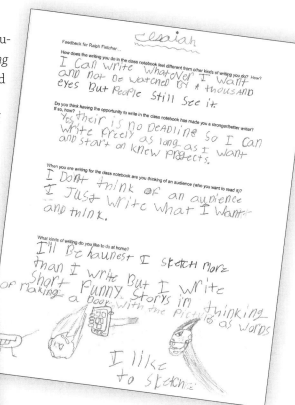

Figure 7.2:
Isaiah's response to my survey questions

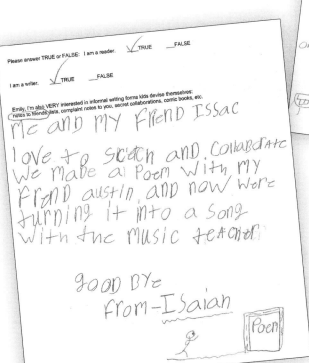

53

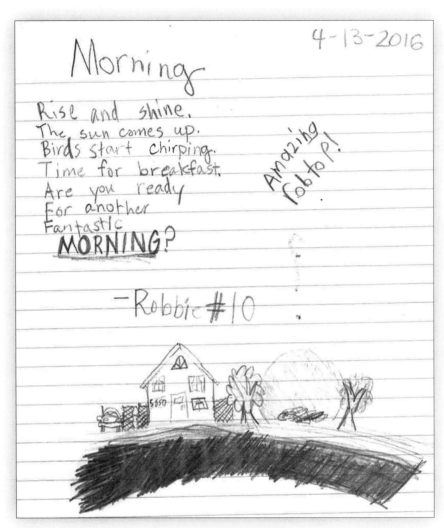

Figure 7.3: Robbie's poem

wonder by valuing it in school. One way we can do this is to invite children to keep wonder journals—to record and share their daily wonders and let their questions, observations and reflections guide our teaching."

When Georgia did a Skype visit with Emily's class, she told students how important it is to devote time to wondering about the world. Many of Emily's students have chosen to devote a specific notebook to wondering.

"I think the biggest impact was the energy and motivation to write because they had choice in what to wonder about, time to pursue it, and opportunity to explore," Emily says. "Nothing was 'published' from this. We celebrated our wonderings through collaborative conversations. Writers would bring their notebooks down and share what they were writing about. We always had something to write with just in case we needed to jot an idea/question from fellow writers. The topics that kids were wondering/writing about ranged from inquiring about the Mayans and Aztecs to why Kenya is considered one of the safer places to seek refuge in Africa to why hermit crabs stay inside their shells."

Popcorn and Poetry Fridays

This is an opportunity for casual conversation about poetry and to share poems students were inspired to write. Because poetry is not included in the Common Core State Standards, many teachers have stopped devoting much time to it. Poetry made a huge difference in Emily's classroom.

"From the very beginning students were reading so much poetry and realized there was so much more to this beautiful genre than silliness and rhymes," Emily says. "Readers were immediately inspired to be poets themselves. Children started trying things out like the poets they were reading. Because so many were seeing themselves as poets, it spread quickly to all of us seeing ourselves as poets. There's so much freedom in poetry that many children saw it as their entry points into becoming writers."

A Class Blog

Julieanne Harmatz teaches fifth grade in San Pedro, California. In recent years she has set up a class blog where her students could post their writing. She started the blog about four years ago.

"I grew so much as a writer by blogging, and getting feedback from other teachers," she says. "I wanted my students to have that same support from their peers."

Julieanne gives her kids fifteen minutes per day to either blog, or respond to an entry created by another kid in class. The blog posts include all kinds of writing: lists to describe themselves; movie reviews; comics; stories about cell phones, video games, pets, siblings, friendships, or fears of going to middle school (toward the end of the year); and poetry. I asked Julieanne if she established any rules or requirements.

"They couldn't include their names, or photos of themselves (district rules for safety)," she says. "My only other rule was that they be kind to each other. Beyond that, I gave them freedom and no requirements."

When I surveyed Julieanne's class I asked the students: "Do you think having the opportunity to write on the classroom blog has made you a stronger/better writer? If so, how?"

Yes: 22

No (or not sure): 6

"Yes because it gets me stronger in all areas," one student wrote. "And I can choose whatever kind of writing I want instead of all of us doing the same one as a class."

I asked: "How does the writing you do for the blog feel different from other kinds of writing you do?" Here are some responses:

- "You get to write anything you want, and in writing workshop you have to write about informational stuff. The blog writing is more creative, and it's about stuff that's really happening."

- "It feels different because on the blog you express your life and your feelings. Also on the blog you are welcome to write your imagination away. What I like is when they comment nice things. It makes you feel good."

Another student agreed.

- "It feels good to know that someone else than your teacher will see it. And I like how we can write whatever we have on our mind."

In other words, kids respond to the blog because it's *personal*, they have a real *audience*, and they have genuine *choice*. Students feel like they can choose their subjects, and express themselves in whatever way they desire.

"The blog is their playground," Julieanne told me. "I feel that it's critical because (writing program) offers so little choice. I want my kids to find a space where they can love writing on their own terms."

I asked Julieanne if her class participation in the blog had brought any unexpected surprises.

"When I have surveyed my students about writing, I discovered that many students didn't see blogging as writing," notes Julieanne. "Which speaks volumes. As fifth graders most have had five years of (writing program), and that's what writing is for many of them."

Writing workshops have become more academic and constricted, but many other teachers around the country are working hard to create a more open, student-centered, choice-based, and responsive writing classroom. They utilize a variety of ideas, some familiar, some new.

The Writer's Notebook

"You didn't invent the writer's notebook, Dad!" my son once reminded me.

"True dat," I cheerfully replied. Which made him groan.

Writer's notebooks have been around since long before I was born. And yet I have written three books about this concept, so perhaps I can be forgiven for feeling a bit proprietary. The writer's notebook is a huge part of my creative process. As I wrote in *Breathing In, Breathing Out* (1996a), the writer's notebook gives me a quiet place to catch my breath and begin writing. (See resource list in Appendix.)

On countless occasions I have seen the magic that can happen when a teacher and students embrace this idea. The writer's notebook may not be *the* writing tool, but it certainly is *a* writing tool every teacher should consider. True, it's only a blank book, but those pages give kids a unique opportunity to find their stride as writers. The writer's notebook is a high-comfort, low-risk place to compose. Those conditions create a hothouse for writing.

In recent years I've observed a growing tendency to take the wildness out of the notebook. In subtle ways some teachers have begun to annex it, to assert influence and claim it as their own. I've even heard of teachers who sometimes give notebook homework: "Tonight I'd like you to write five compound sentences in your notebook."

Please don't. Kids have so little in school that they really own! The writer's notebook is one of those rare things that should belong to them. The notebook is a writing greenbelt—let's keep it wild. Like any natural area, it thrives on benign neglect.

Impromptu Shares

Many teachers have schemed to find ways of getting more kids to share what they have written. Blair, a fourth-grade teacher in Texas, invites her students to share excerpts from their writer's notebooks. She named this ritual Reading into the Circle.

"The entries they read aloud give other kids ideas for what they might do in their own notebooks," Blair says.

Debbie Goldsworthy, a fifth-grade teacher in Michigan's Upper Peninsula, schedules a monthly celebration she calls Word to the Mic where students in grades 3–5 can share their writing in the library during recess and lunch in front of peers in the library.

"I have a microphone and an amp," Debbie says. "I decorate the tables with centerpieces. The featured writers' table has a real tablecloth. I place a large marquee just outside of the library listing names of the featured writers. Students who walk by read their names and know they are reading to others in a type of open mike setting. I try to make it special and encourage students to share writing—not as a contest, but as a shared experience. If there's time, I share some of my own writing."

Teachers like Debbie are helping kids know what it feels like to connect with a real audience. Not only that, but they are letting kids discover that writing can be fun.

Other intriguing ideas include:

- Free choice Fridays: Students get carte blanche to write about anything, in any genre they choose

- "Morning Pages": This is an idea gleaned from *The Artist's Way: A Spiritual Path to Higher Creativity* by Julia Cameron (1992). In this book the author suggests several exercises including Morning Pages, which you sit down and just write a few pages first thing in morning. "There is no wrong way to do Morning Pages—they are not high art," Cameron explains. "They aren't even 'writing.' They are about anything and everything that crosses your mind—and they are for your eyes only."

I talked to several teachers who are experimenting with Morning Pages in their classroom. They see them as a way to promote quantity, fluency, and to outrun the censor that lives inside so many writers, young and old.

Home Writer's Notebooks ("Spy Notebooks")

Kids have a special writer's notebook for home.

Writing Workouts

"My students have a 'writing workout' assignment where they turn in two or three paragraphs on any topic they choose," says Melissa Leisner, a seventh-grade teacher. "The purpose is to help them develop fluency."

In a better world, teachers might not have to create authentic writing opportunities for their students that are special or out of the ordinary. That need would be satisfied by the writing workshop. But in today's scripted world, many teachers feel like the formal workshop writing isn't enough.

"The program we use is quite challenging and can turn writing into something that is just hard," Julieanne Harmatz says. "I want my students to write with few constraints, with ample time, and no grading. I want to give them the opportunity to find their voice—without having to use a checklist."

I commend Julieanne and all the other teachers who are working hard to create the kind of environment kids need to flourish into strong writers. These brave souls find themselves rowing against a strong current. These initiatives, and many others like them, represent courageous attempts to give young writers more choice and voice, more of a stake in their work—more oxygen. Administrators and parents may not always understand the value of these efforts, but I certainly do.

Classroom notebooks, wonder notebooks, writer's notebooks, impromptu shares: check, check, check, check.

And yet.

Although the writing opportunities described in this chapter and the previous one are undeniably rich, they are almost all teacher-structured, at least at the outset. I'm equally interested in the greenbelt writing that kids invent on their own.

Chocolate Café menu and invite by Sarah and Sadie

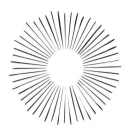

CHAPTER 8

Feral Writing

....

feral (adjective): in a wild state, especially after escape from captivity or domestication

....

The two brothers had dinner with their parents at a Chinese restaurant. When the meal ended, the waiter brought a little tray containing pineapple chunks along with four fortune cookies. They all did the ritual thing, cracking open the cookies and reading their fortunes aloud. After Dad paid the bill, they walked out to their car. The boys were *not* looking forward to the two-hour drive to Grandma's house.

"My fortune said *You shall live a lively life*," sighed Nathan, the younger of the two brothers. "So why do we have to do this boring drive?"

"Hey, I know what we should do!" Max hissed softly. "We should write our own fortunes! Like the ones in the restaurant!"

"Yeah!" Nathan pumped his fist. "Let's do it!"

Max rummaged around the console between the two seats until he found a pad of large sticky notes. He grabbed the pad, located a pen that actually worked, and the boys set to work.

"*May you never eat black-bean chili before going to a movie in a crowded theatre*," Max whispered. Then he added: "Because of the farts!"

"Yeah!" Laughter.

"Listen to this!" Nathan said. "*May the toilet paper never run out while you're sitting on the thrown.*"

Max giggled. "That's not how you spell *throne* but, yeah, that's wicked funny!"

Mom swiveled around and eyed them suspiciously.

"What are you guys doing?"

"We're writing our own fortunes," Max explained. "Like fortune cookie fortunes, only better."

Nathan grinned. "Yeah, a *lot* better."

"Well, I hope they're not inappropriate," Mom murmured.

Max laughed. "Oh, they're inappropriate, all right! But it's OK, Mom. Don't worry."

When an author comes to visit the school, students buy a book and get it autographed. During the book fair, parents give their kids money so they can buy books. When kids go to the library, they take out at least one book.

We expect that our children, and our students, will always have a book they're engrossed in. Independent reading has numerous benefits, helping kids develop fluency, stamina, and comprehension. Most important: it helps them develop a connection between books and pleasure. They discover via direct experience that reading is fun.

Shouldn't the same thing be true of writing? I believe kids should be writing all the time. They *are* writing all the time, in school and out, for reasons that are practical as well as whimsical. When I was a kid I wrote tiny notes and inserted them into tiny acorns I had hollowed out. I attached these acorns to helium balloons and sent my messages into the sky, wondering who might find and read them in some faraway land.

The writing bug—the inclination to jot something down—persists today. Kids scribble notes, text, create lyrics, make lists, compose letters, Snapchat, tweet, post status updates on Facebook . . . (see Figure 8.1).

Students may not always consider such activity "writing"; my research suggests that they often do not. Indeed, the confining conditions that surround school writing have been removed. There's no adult looking over their shoulder, prodding them to complete it. There's no writing conference, no multiple drafts, no mandatory revisions. There's no standard, anchor paper, or rubric to follow. No editing checklist, due date, or impending grade. But for many students, this low-stakes writing will have a higher impact than any of the "school writing" they produce.

When kids choose to write on their own they do so for many different reasons/purposes. My oldest son wrote contracts, stipulating complicated agreements (often involving baseball or Magic cards) between himself and his brother Adam. My kids filled dozens of notebooks, and they did most of this writing at home, on their own initiative. JoAnn and I take no credit in this; we attribute this to the strong, passionate writing teachers (Ann Marie Corgill, Steve Tullar, Heather Brown, and Linda Rief, among others) they were lucky to have.

When Robert was in third grade he and his friend Max spent months working on Fighting Fruit, a series inspired by the *Redwall* books. The boys concocted a series of characters, each one with its own personality and, of course, favorite weapon. In typical boy fashion, these books included lots of vio-

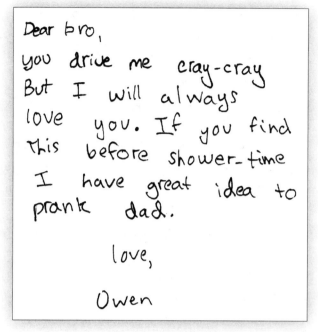

Figure 8.1: Note from Owen to his brother

lence, zany humor, wordplay, and action-packed illustrations. The characters included Pear of Aces, Melon Choly, Exploding Eggplant, and Kamikaze Kiwi.

When I attended West Islip High School, on Long Island, New York, a group of students were angry at how the school was being run. They decided to create an underground newspaper: *The Bloodthirsty Wolverine*. It contained jokes, parodies, diatribes, and scathing reviews of certain teachers. Some contributors included only their initials; the brave ones signed their full names. Believe me, no text in that school was scrutinized more closely. The *Bloodthirsty Wolverine* got banned by the school administration, which only increased its cache.

I titled this chapter "Feral Writing." The term *feral* refers to an animal that was once domesticated but has returned to its wild, untamed state. I believe this concept applies here. As the workshop has become more domesticated, kids thirst for opportunities that allow them to (re)discover the raw, untamed power of writing.

Backup/Independent Writing Projects

A few years ago Emily Callahan read Katie Wood Ray's important book *Study Driven*. Emily found one concept especially intriguing: backup, or independent writing projects. Katie describes backup work as "kid-sponsored, often recklessly wonderful writing that may not be very good but is something students have chosen to work on because the idea of writing it gives them energy" (2006, 154). This is a rich sentence, and one that's worth unpacking. Note the way Katie describes independent writing:

- "recklessly wonderful"
- "may not be not very good" (True! The quality of such writing will not necessarily be exemplary.)
- "something students have chosen to work on" (Choice)
- "the idea of writing it gives them energy." (Not just writing it, but the *idea* of writing it. So kids are thinking about the project even when they're not actually working on it.)

An examination of backup work can be found here: https://twowriting teachers.org/2014/05/08/independent-writing-back-up-work/.

Emily had never really considered this before, and decided to give it a try. Backup work quickly became a big part of her writing classroom.

"We were *big* into backup work this year, so kids wrote informally almost daily," Emily says. "My students always had something going on in addition to the specific genre study we were working on. Kids would write (and lots of time would join forces) plays, fantasy stories, series of stories, comedies, songs . . . A project like this may not turn into anything formal. It may never get published. But the fact that it's there, and they can go to it during choice time, has created so much energy and motivation when it comes to writing." (See Figure 8.2.)

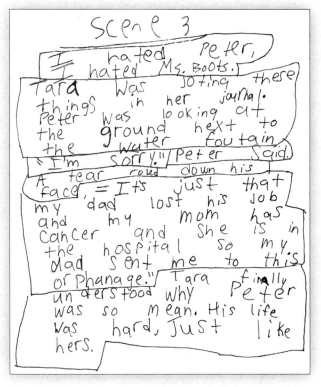

Figure 8.2: Student example from Emily's class

Kathleen Sokolowski teaches third grade in Farmingdale, New York. The kids in her classroom did a great deal of informal writing. Often this writing spilled out of the school day and got completed at home (see Figure 8.3).

Figure 8.3a–d: Autobiography by Dia'Monie

One of Kathleen's students, a boy named Brendan, made a comic called *Super Pig*, a work inspired by the Captain Underpants series (see Figure 8.4).

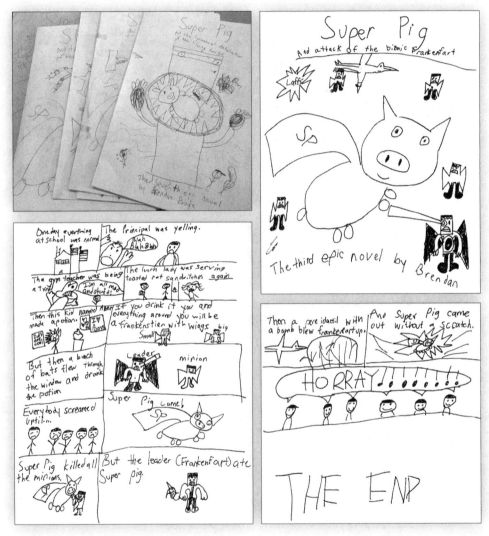

Figure 8.4a-d: *Super Pig* by Brendan

"I really value their informal writing," Kathleen told me. "I think it shows agency, ownership. It helps them write with voice. These students see themselves as writers."

When I surveyed teachers I asked them: "What kinds of informal writing do your students do?"

"Every year I have a group of kids who draw at lunch," Julieanne Harmatz, a fifth-grade teacher, told me. "They walk off with their spiral notebooks and pens to talk and draw. Manuals (often related to video games) and step-by-step drawing books have come out of that. Just today, two kids came up to me with their 'book idea' (their words) based on their drawings. Each character had a name, magical powers, and a quest."

Karen Huy teaches third grade. She listed a variety of informal writing activities that take place in her class:

- short stories

- poems

- graphic novels

- comic strips

- journals

- diaries

- social media posts (Snapchat and Instagram, mostly)

- directions for games they create

- info books about topics that interest them

- riddles and jokes ("usually beautifully bad ones").

"And there's an assortment of random, unclassifiable texts that defy genre," Karen added. "Sometimes they just write."

Dalila Eckstein reported that her students create:

- comics (on their own and on the computer using Comic Life), or #NaPo WriMo (National Poetry Writing Month)

- slideshows about animals

- persuasive letters to a parent (or to her for a class pet, which happened!)

- writing inspired by favorite books (*Wimpy Kid* series)

- notes to each other

- signs. ("Signs for our classroom including RIP tombstones for our two goldfish that died," Dalila says. "And our Writing Center Manager put an OUT OF ORDER sign on two of the paper bins when we ran out of blank white and colored paper.")

Other teachers I surveyed reported that their students produced a dizzying variety of informal writing, a lively mix of digital and old-school: padlets (I admit I had to look this up), sticky notes to each other, jots in the Jot Lot, letters to the teacher, exit tickets, blogs, posts on Google Classroom, book talks, fan fiction, notes (mean, nice, love), posters, cards, memes, autobiographies and biographies of neighbors, movie-based writing, Google Slide and Apple Keynote presentations, individual blogs, fact books, fan fiction, collaborative plays, long fantasy fiction pieces, raps, songs, poetry, or cell phone texts (see Figure 8.5).

"My students like to draw and write a story about a character," says Bernita Corder, a second-grade teacher. "They often make themselves or their friends the hero. Sometimes they think it is very funny to have a friend or the teacher be eaten or killed by some event, or creature."

Sonja Mangrum teaches eighth grade in Rome, Georgia.

"My students journal and write their own narratives," Sonja told me. She added pointedly: "I know of none who choose to do argumentative or expository writing just for the fun of it."

Figure 8.5: Hyun Su and Liam text about a *Minecraft* server game

Goof-Around Writing

Sometimes when I write I do nothing more than fool around and play, not worrying about punctuation or form or what the piece might eventually become. This is from my writer's notebook:

blue blue blueberry blue

sapphires on bushes

picked beneath a blue moon

sweet blue explosions

on tongue and mouth

buckets of blueberries

for blueberry pancakes

blueberry cake blueberry

cobbler and compote

blueberry pie with darkblue

juices that stain T-shirt & teeth

so many berries in my cereal

they out-vote the Cheerios

oh and did I mention I'm writing

the most delicious poem

with a blueblueblueberry pen

that goes on and on forever

and never reaches

the end

My goof-around writing tends to be highly experimental, and usually doesn't result in a finished product. I once wrote a series of Weather Letters (Tornado writing to Hurricane, for example). Another time I tried making a collection I called Pointless Stories—including one classic tale titled "The Boy Who Swallowed a Parenthesis." I never did anything with this story, but I had flat-out fun writing it. And if writing isn't going to be fun, at least most of the time, what's the point of being a writer?

In a community the greenbelt plays an important role not only for what it is (wild), but also for what it is not (developed). In this chapter, and the two chapters that precede it, I have shared multiple possibilities for greenbelt writing. I want to emphasize that, like an actual greenbelt, such writing needs to have its own distinct identity, one that is different from the genres we cycle through in writing workshop. It must *feel* different to your students. If it doesn't feel different, well, then it's not greenbelt writing.

At the beginning of this chapter I mentioned Katie Wood Ray's idea of backup/independent work. I'm grateful to her for introducing this idea and exploring it so thoughtfully in her book. Katie's a friend of mine, and I have enormous respect for her ideas on writing, so I don't think she'll mind if I pick one small bone with her. She refers to kids' independent writing as "backup writing," but I wonder if that term is accurate. At a rock concert the backup act is the one nobody pays much attention to. It comes on first, when people are still milling around, trying to find their seats. The backup band kills time until the main act—what people paid money for—steps onto the stage. Later, many attendees won't even remember the name of the backup band.

Does this also hold true for writing?

Main event: writing workshop

Backup writing: independent writing

I would submit that this hierarchy should be reversed. Maybe it used to be like this, but as writing workshop has gotten more academic, structured, and formulaic, we are seeing more and more turned-off writers. For this reason, it may not be what they do during writing workshop but while they're engrossed in their independent work—what I am calling greenbelt or feral writing—that will make the difference. Only there will they find the necessary conditions (choice, voice, freedom, engagement, ownership, audience, playfulness) to develop into passionate, capable writers.

Comics by Vinny

Comics by Vinny

CHAPTER 9

I'm-Trying-to-Figure-This-Out Writing

I got an idea for a new professional book—this one, as a matter of fact—but it seemed vague and murky. When this happens, I often find it helpful to kick the idea around with a trusted friend, so I contacted Katie Wood Ray, an editor for Heinemann. Technically Katie was not my editor, but I didn't think she would mind batting the idea around with me. I zipped her an email.

> Hi Katie,
> Could I ask you, off the official record, for your reaction to a book idea? I value your input as an author and writing person. Let me know.

She promptly responded:

> I think off the record, yes, I'd be delighted to react to an idea. Send it along. My lips are sealed and I'd relish the opportunity to think a little with you.

I wrote:

> OK, here's my elevator pitch.
> Many teachers see writing as something that must be correct and corrected. But isn't writing really a tool for thinking? Smart people use

it that way all the time. I think there should be a book extolling the virtues of informal writing. I had the idea that book itself should be written informally—which would be fun. I envision sections/chunks/chapters on:

Texts, Blogs, Social media posts, Notes (the kind of notes kids pass in class), Writers notebooks, Diaries, Write-alouds, Quick-writes, Vents/rants, Exploratory writing.

Right now my working title is *JOT, JOT, JOT: The Power of Informal Writing*. Maybe there's already a book out there on this. Maybe this idea doesn't have enough heft and should be an article. What do you think?

Katie wrote a thoughtful reply, one too lengthy to post here, though I'll include a few snippets:

My first, gut reaction is: What fun (especially when I see the first three things on the list). But I do have lots of questions. I think I'm going to bullet them because it's easier for me to think them out that way (they may overlap).

. . .

I usually think of "informal" as referring to the style/tone of writing rather than *low-risk/low-stakes writing*. In other words, a writer might draft and revise extensively and on a piece that still has what would be considered an informal rather than formal tone. So I'm not quite sure which aspect of that word you're getting at. Informal in style or informal in process? Both?

. . .

To me, the verb "jot" doesn't really capture the range of intensities involved in these different kinds of writing. Jot feels very quick, very low intensity to me. If I'm thinking hard in writing, as with say exploratory writing, I feel like I'm doing something more than jotting.

I felt I had hit pay dirt—she really got me thinking! I replied:

Thanks! Whoa, you delved deeper into this than I expected. *JOT, JOT, JOT* is a play on dot, dot, dot. Duh, I guess that's probably obvious.

I believe that ANY kind of writing is valuable, esp. the most casual kind of jottings, scribblings, written ramblings, marginalia, scrawlings, knock-offs, scratchings, bang-outs. . . .

By informal, I mean stress-free writing that is not intended to be graded or corrected. Low-stakes. When I'm involved in exploratory writing, yeah, I'm thinking hard, but I'm not stressing about spelling or grammar. I wonder if, as educators, we really understand that. Sure, we might let kids talk their way into an understanding of a subject. But as soon as students start writing, well, I'm afraid we narrow our eyes and begin assessing. Which is exactly what we shouldn't do.

Next Katie replied:

So my brain didn't get that *Jot, Jot, Jot* was like dot, dot, dot. Slow, I guess. But I do get it and it is very clever. :)

I just think there is a lot of potential here. *I am already in a different place in my thinking just by reading your thoughts and then responding to them.* (italic text mine)

I was going to title this chapter "Writing to Learn," but I don't think that's wholly accurate. Consider my back-and-forth dialogue with Katie Ray that begins this chapter. Those conversations formed the early roots of this book. It has changed substantially since then, but that early dialogue was crucial. It's not so much that I was learning; I already had the knowledge inside me. Rather, I was clarifying my vision, figuring out what I might want to explore.

Note the tenor of this writing. Although our dialogue is on-task and focused, it also feels informal and colloquial. Both of us are comfortable using expressions and shorthand. This writing may not be polished enough for consumption by the general public, but it certainly served its main purpose here by pushing my thinking.

A few years ago I met Brian Cambourne, author of *Conditions for Learning*, a foundational text that has profoundly influenced educational thinking around the world. I was eager to get Brian's thoughts on this subject, so I sent him an email interview.

"Fifty years of naturalistic observation has convinced me that the majority of teachers subconsciously frame writing as a medium for communication," Cambourne told me. "Very few frame it as a medium for thinking, learning, and/or solving problems."

Cambourne believes that teachers need to embed messages about reading and writing they want their students to internalize. These messages should include:

- "Writing is primarily a tool of thinking, learning, and problem-solving."
- "Being an effective learner, thinker, and problem-solver will allow you to experience and acquire the good things of life and avoid the pitfalls and perils."

- "Using writing this way is easy, enjoyable, worth learning, and can be fun."

Cambourne goes on to argue that teachers must create opportunities for their students to observe demonstrations of writing being used in this way.

Many writers strive to create literature—poems, essays, fiction, and the like—and that is certainly a worthy endeavor. But creating literature comprises only a small slice of all the writing that gets done in the world. More typically we use writing to puzzle things out.

In this chapter I'm making a sharp distinction between these two kinds of writing: writing to communicate, and writing to think, learn, solve problems. This distinction is important because differing audiences bring different expectations. If I'm writing a letter to an editor, or crafting a poem for a poetry anthology, I know the writing must be accurate and correct. But if I'm jotting notes, musing to myself, or emailing a pal (as I was with Katie Wood Ray), I know that correctness matters far less than meaning.

We use writing-to-think every day in our lives. In recent weeks I found myself making various lists:

- Guests for a possible summer party. From this master list, we made separate sublists for smaller groups of individuals that might work better as a dinner party.

- Packing list for my photographic trip to Costa Rica. Actually this is a series of lists: photo gear, clothing, and medicine. These lists begat still other lists, reminding me what items (breathable rain gear and so on) I still needed to purchase.

- When my wife was offered a job at the University of Alabama Birmingham, we tried to tease out the pros and cons of such a move. To do so we collaborated on a PMI list:

Pluses	Minuses	Interesting
Great job	Far from family	Exciting new place
Mild winters	Harder flight connections	Cultural experience for kids
	Hot summers	Chance to explore the South

Creating a list like this, and the discussion it required, helped us make the final decision about whether or not JoAnn should take the position.

This chapter is about tentative writing, musing, thinking aloud on paper. I've included it rather late in this book, but that fact shouldn't be taken to suggest that I consider it an afterthought. I don't. In fact I'd go so far as to say that 75 percent of all the writing kids do in school should be this kind of I'm-trying-to-figure-this-out writing.

So what does this kind of writing look like in the classroom? It would include notes, written reactions, quick-writes, summaries, what-I'm-thinking-right-now. It might include "Dash Facts" for primary writers where kids involved in a nonfiction study are encouraged to jot down one or two facts about the subject.

It might also include the Exploratory Notebook, an idea I wrote about in my book *Making Nonfiction from Scratch* (2015). The Exploratory Notebook acts as a container to hold kids' tentative thinking on a nonfiction topic. The concept could be expanded and used in other subjects as well.

We should remember that this kind of greenbelt writing is meaning-based, not meant for public consumption. It's private and personal. It's not presentational, and it shouldn't be treated as such. Writing teachers need to think carefully about how to create conditions that will encourage and not squelch it. This starts with bringing the right mind-set or attitude to such writing. Your students will be encouraged to generate more of such writing if you:

- consider it as thinking-on-paper
- read it with interest (though don't feel like you have to read all of it)
- share excerpts out loud, if appropriate, and with the students' permission
- view it as a window into the students' thinking.

Remember that learning is a moving train. What a student thinks today does not indicate where he'll be next week.

Model your own writing of this kind.

Don't:

- correct it
- grade it
- assess it
- require a certain minimum number of pages
- comment on messy handwriting.

Also, we should be wary of turning this kind of writing into tedious busywork. The writing should serve the task—not the other way around. As soon as such writing becomes burdensome, it ceases being helpful. Sometimes writing really does belabor the issue; the best way to communicate is to put down the pencil and just talk.

Writing helps us discover what we know. Writing is different from talking. When we jot something down, we distill its essence; it becomes part of us; we own it in a new way. Writing has an uncanny way of getting our mental juices flowing, as happened to me through my correspondence with Katie. I envision classrooms where kids are doing lots of this kind of greenbelt writing on a daily basis, but it should be voluntary. And we should encourage fluency. (If you have students who struggle with a pen, try to get them a keyboard.) Most important, it should feel casual and stress-free. This is low-stakes writing all the way.

> Lesson 1: How to do a front roll
> Step 1: squat down with your hands on the mat.
> Step 2: tuck your head in and push of with your legs.
>
> Lesson 2: How to do a front flip
> Step 1: Bend your knees with your hands in front of you.
> Step 2: Push off and kick your legs up and over from behind you.
> PS. It is okay if you fall on your back or your bottom.
>
> Lesson 3: Backwards Roll
> Step 1: sit on your bottom with your legs out in front of you and lean forward.
> Step 2: Lean back and bring your legs over your head all the way.
> PS. you will land on your knees.

How To Do a Forward Roll by Mi Ae

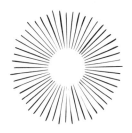

CHAPTER 10

The Reluctant Writer

Greenbelt writing will solve all the major problems you face in the classroom. It will deepen your students' reading comprehension, enhance their moral development, and allow them to practice important study skills. Not only that, but it will reduce stress, lower your blood pressure, and strengthen your marriage.

OK, maybe not. But here's an upside, and this one's legit. It turns out that greenbelt writing can help with one problem that every teacher faces—the kid with a serious aversion to writing. This is a benefit I didn't foresee when I began exploring this topic.

Meet the reluctant writer. Often, though not always, this student is a boy. He's not very communicative, though his body language (bored eyes, vacant expression, slumped down in his seat) speaks volumes. While your other students settle into their writing, the reluctant writer sits there fidgeting, blank eyes floating over a blank piece of paper. After fifteen minutes, he's looking to escape. Count on him to ask if he can go to the bathroom, and vanish for twenty minutes, until finally you have to send a posse to drag him back.

Jayce was such a student in Terry Stoufer's second-grade class.

"Jayce avoided writing," Terry told me. "He would write very little. It usually took days for him to complete even a small amount of writing. He didn't show any pleasure or engagement."

I was struck by the data Terry used to assess Jayce's strengths and weaknesses as a writer: behavior (avoidance), quantity of writing, pleasure, and engagement. In the mid-autumn, Terry introduced blogging to her students, and Jayce really took to it. Here are a few samples of his blog posts. (Remember: these are from a second-grade student.)

Oct. 14, 2015 Hi Amy krouse rosenthal. my name is Jayce we read your book duck! Rabbit! I think it is a rabbit. I do like your writing.

- -

Nov. 4, 2015 I'm not perfect at swimming. I'm not perfect at catching foot balls. I'm not perfect at riding my bike on rocks. I'm not perfect at getting distracted. I'm not perfect at throwing balls. Not perfect means not good at.

- -

April 11, 2016 Dear mrs. Lofton,

our class wants miss Jena to come to our class for some reasons. She is kind and funny to all of us, she helped us be okay with mistakes, she would sometimes use dogs for important lessons, she would help us with being not perfect.

Sincinerely,

Jayce

- -

April 26, 2016

It looks fat

It is fast

It was sunny

It was dark

It was sparkly

It sounds weird

It sounds cool

Why is it stormy

Why is it rainy

I felt good

I felt bad

I felt mad

Why

Why

Why

Sounds

Sounds

Sounds

I asked Terry how Jayce was able to make such dramatic strides in his writing. She suggested four things:

1. "He started to see himself as a writer. He had an 'I can't' attitude but that changed due to positive feedback. I made it a point to celebrate what he did, and not focus on what he didn't do."

2. "We were involved in projects that gave him an audience. He started to see that what he wrote was being read. He had a purpose and real readers. It appeared to empower him when he saw comments outside of our classroom on his blog. At times on the blog we were writing to a global audience."

3. "Early in the year, due to scheduling and school expectations, I didn't run a regular writing workshop. As a result my writing instruction felt haphazard. After observing Jayce and others, I realized that I needed to go back to what I knew worked. Jayce definitely changed when that instruction changed. There he had more time to write and experiment. And choice was a key to his

growth. He loves racing and he chose to write about that most of the time. Through conferencing with him I could encourage him and ask questions that helped him to see his possibilities."

4. "Jayce has a physical handicap in his hands. I believe he found it easier to type on the blog. And I noticed that he started to apply workshop lessons to his blogging."

Terry acknowledges that Jayce is not completely out of the woods. "He still struggles with writing but he approaches it with a different attitude," she says. "I see his voice beginning to develop. He writes so much more now, and his word choice shows he is seeing the power of words."

I heard similar stories from many other teachers. Here's a sampling:

Jennifer Erickson, third-grade teacher: "My struggling writers have demonstrated the most significant impact on their growth through informal writing, as it provides them with the opportunity to play with words, use their imagination, make mistakes, share their successes, and receive feedback from classmates."

Kathleen Masone, fourth-grade teacher: "I have a student this year who is a perfectionist. She struggled with writing in the beginning of the year mainly because she couldn't get past the visual perfection of her writing on the page. Informal writing has helped her grow out of her comfort zone and realize that writing can and should be messy from time to time. She has learned that a writer's notebook is a great place to experiment. Her writing has really developed (detail, voice)."

Heather Lambright, fourth-grade teacher: "One of my students has been identified with a disability in writing this year. However, he loves to work on his *Minecraft* story. We use this story—his informal writing—as a buy-in and as a tool to teach the lessons we want him to work on. This has helped him to foster maybe not a love but at least a *like* for writing, even though it is his weakest area."

Jen Bearden, second-grade teacher: "I have three kids in particular who, even by first or second grade already believed they were not writers. They saw no need to write, and had no desire to learn more. Giving them freedom to do whatever they wanted and to 'play' with writing made them more willing and able to try new things when I needed them to later on in our work. The same was true with countless fifth graders (whose certainty that they were *bad* writers or that they didn't like writing was even more pronounced). I found that with older students, they had had so many years where writing was merely an isolated focus on grammar and a time when the teacher told them exactly what to do that it was no wonder they found it so unpleasant. Most of these were boys (although there have been girls, too), and it was again the freedom to play and experiment—especially with pictures—that helped them become more interested, and allowed them to trust me when I pushed them to do harder things."

Isabel Tuliao, fourth-grade teacher: "Zach was in my class last year. He would quietly call my attention to pages of short stories he created at home. It was mostly fantasy with lots of adventure and action. He really prided himself in being able to share a piece of writing with his teacher. It was through these writings that we were able to make a connection that made our work in the workshop more rewarding."

Christy Constande, second-grade teacher: "Recently I had a student who could never think of anything to write. He would completely shut down. I tried him on the computer and that helped some. I figured that until I could get him to feel like a writer, I didn't need to bother with genre writing. So I let him just write informally in his Spy Journal. He made the most progress of any of my writers last year."

Amanda Morrison, fifth-grade teacher: "I have a student who is a very low reader/writer. At the beginning of the year, his writing was at least two grade levels behind, especially in the category of elaboration. His writing sounded very robotic. A few months ago, he brought an Ellen DeGeneres book to school that his mom got for him (it gave me quite the chuckle too!). He was *so* interested in this book. After he finished it he spent the next few weekends typing up his own autobiography. When he arrived at school with several published copies, he was confidently handing them out to classmates and teachers to read. Although the writing was riddled with grammar, spelling, and punctuation errors, it was full of voice and humor, which his classroom writing lacked. Although he is still performing below grade level in writing, the growth he has made this year is evident and his confidence has really grown as well."

Julieanne Harmatz had a student named Bolu in her fifth-grade class. He started the year as a turned-off writer. The physical act of writing was difficult for him. He avoided it. But he took to blogging.

"The keyboard helped," Julieanne told me. "And blogging was a natural for him—it allowed him to express his voice. Bolu learned to use spell check features of Google Docs. He learned to move his writing from Docs to the blog and upload pictures. Writing for his peers was also a huge incentive."

The milk

by Bolu on Nov. 24, 2015

One day my dad came back from work. And brought some milk. I was like "finally we have milk." So that ment we could open the fruit Lupe. I was thinking of that all day. Once I had a chance to open the fruit Lupe. My dad said that I could not open the fruit Lupe until I finish the frosted flakes. I was like but why. He said he did not want to waste it. After like three weeks the frosted flakes were finished. So I opened the fruit Lupe. But I needed milk. But the only milk that was in the fridge was silk milk. But the thing is I didn't know silk milk was almond milk. So I put in the bowl and ate the cereal. Right when I put it in my mouth. I spit it back out. It was terrible. And I learned to always check what kind of milk I should use.

Bolu received the following responses to his post.

Joe: "I like almond milk!?!?!? Y U NO LIKE IT?!?!?!"

Enrique: "It was roten! ive had close encounters too."

Sherry: "Hilarious. I did that once before. We bought almond milk accidentally."

Owen: "That does sound quite like a traumatic experience with the Fruit-Loops. I have had the same first-world problems as you too. My family does not purchase almond milk. Have you had any other experiences that relate to this one?"

Mehlum: "Wow, that must be rough because of the bad taste of almond milk. I wonder how adults like almond milk because it tastes bad a lot. Well, I guess you learned a lesson not to EVER drink almond milk with cereal. Did you ever finish that bowl? Or did you just throw it out in disgust? Whenever I hate something my mom makes me finish it."

Nicole: "So funny. I really liked the ending. Good closing your story off. Have you ever tried Silk Milk before? Did it taste horrible too?"

Note that not one of these responses mentioned the many mechanical errors in Bolu's post. Nicole commends him for the craft of his ending, the way he "closes off" his story. His other readers responded to the heart—the meaning—of what he wrote. This is the way we naturally respond to very young children when they are learning to talk. We rarely correct or fixate on their errors. Instead, we respond to what they are trying to say.

The "help" reluctant writers receive is usually highly structured directions given during one-on-one conferring. I've observed that often these students are channeled into formulaic outlines with a rigid structure. Often the student is directed to fill out a story map, graphic organizer, or cluster web. Teachers watch closely as he slowly forms the letters to create one sentence. Most of the "help" focuses almost exclusively on grammar and mechanics. In this chapter, I am suggesting we take a different approach, one that may seem counterintuitive. Instead of giving reluctant writers more structure, let's give them *more freedom*. Invite students to try out any of the writing types detailed in Chapters 6 and 7, and especially the ideas found in Chapter 8. Encourage:

- free-writing

- journal writing

- writing in a favorite genre—nonfiction, poetry, fantasy

- collaborative writing—invite them to write with a buddy

- humor

- obsessions

- edgy writing.

When you work with a reluctant writer, it's helpful to expand your definition of writing to include drawing, sketching, and doodling. The part of our brain that deals with images is different from the part that deals with language. Drawing can be a soothing, centering activity. I've observed that for many students drawing acts as rehearsal for writing.

When we consider the term *reluctant writer*, we may picture an outlier, an unusual case. But in today's restrictive writing atmosphere, the reluctant writer may be more the rule than the exception.

"When my students arrive in my classroom, they are often reluctant writers who have been forced to write five-paragraph essays for every genre they have been exposed to," Conchetta Marrucci told me. "They are stymied by previous writing experiences."

I'm excited by the notion that encouraging more informal, low-stakes writing might jump-start these young writers. Still, it's important to remember that the reluctant writer is not a monolithic type. These are individual students, quirky kids who often struggle with multiple issues. Often English is not their first language. There's no one-size-fits-all cure, strategy, or fix to help them make the breakthrough into writing fluency. Indeed I spoke with several teachers who were intrigued by the possible benefits of informal writing, but injected a note of caution.

"I don't believe that free-writing helps build stamina, but I do see it increasing enjoyment," says Kimberelle Martin, a fourth-grade teacher in Texas. "It will still take a strong teacher to help students make the connection that what they are doing is actual writing—to be read by others—for them to feel like they are writers."

I talked to a few other teachers who weren't sold on the idea that greenbelt writing would translate into stronger formal, classroom writing.

"Maybe the most important thing about informal writing is that it helps kids see themselves as writers," says Carrie Brotemarkle, a reading teacher in Virginia. "I have one student who is a struggling reader and writer (according to grade-level standards). But he sees himself as a writer and spends time at home working on a comic book series. I don't know that this work has helped improve his writing at school, but I do believe that his home writing has had an impact on his confidence as a writer."

Karen Huy, a third-grade teacher, told me: "I don't know if informal writing increases their enjoyment of writing, but it does let them live writing in a way that they find enjoyable, meaningful, and worth spending time on. Even my most reluctant classroom writers do write informally, which normalizes writing as an activity that is present throughout their lives. I try to point out, without getting pedantic, that this writing is writing. Before I can even get reluctant writers to regard themselves as writers, I have to get them to see all of their many forms of writing as writing."

These thoughtful comments, and many others like it, further pushed my thinking. One teacher, who chose to remain anonymous, said to me: "Informal writing builds stamina but, more important: students who have lost their way as writers begin to see themselves as writers again."

In the past fifteen years numerous studies have shown that getting kids out of school and giving them contact with wild, green spaces can have significant benefits, especially to those who suffer from ADHD. The same principle applies here. Reluctant writers will benefit from prolonged visits to the writing greenbelt. Encourage them to go play in the woods (see Figure 10.1).

by Enrique on Jan. 21, 2016 (Julieanne Harmatz's class)

my first city in minecraft i ketpt seartcing for the best place

then finaly i came across a desert a wide open space it started

ona hill side the first villagers came then more! i was exited so

i built a hotel and then the hotel came over populaed so i bult

more houses but when thanksgiveing came around i bulit a

chandeler a big table and cup of hot coco and even a turkey!

Figure 10.1: Blog entry about *Minecraft* by Enrique

it ws awsome! i had police as iorn golems and when a scince experment went wrong a canyon came rabits came! and that came it became rabbit canyon then one day a villager came with the name dr.trayrus over his head!!!

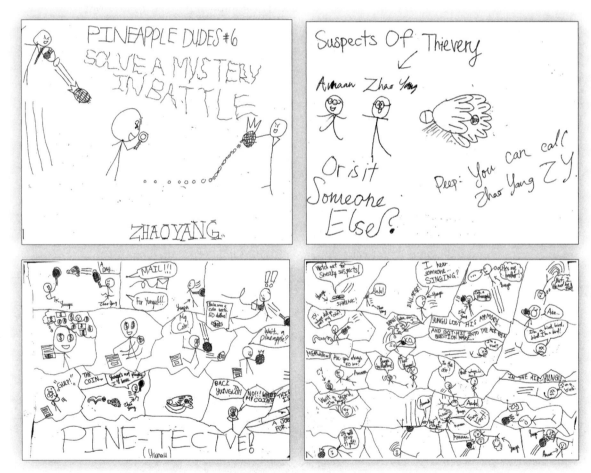

Pineapple Dudes by Zhao

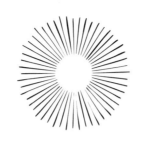

The Big Picture

A central goal
of school should
be to engender a
love of writing
and reading.

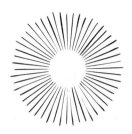

CHAPTER 12

Ralph on Ralph: A Self-Interview

Q: Chapter 11 is *very* short. I think it's the shortest chapter I've ever seen. No offense but . . . did you just kind of forget to write the rest?

A: Nope. I wanted to keep it short. Sometimes you water down your message when you do too much explaining.

Q: You didn't cite a source for Chapter 11. Who are you quoting?

A: Me.

Q (after a pause)**:** Um, I'm not sure you can do that.

A: Well, I did. I wrote it because it's true. And because it's clear we are not doing enough to meet that goal. The way writing is taught today, kids aren't developing a love of writing. They're just not. We can do better. We *have* to do better.

Q: You're using *greenbelt writing* as a catch-all phrase for various kinds of informal, low-stakes writing.

A: Yes. I'm talking about all the writing kids choose to do outside the writing workshop. Stuff that is student-initiated. But the term *low-stakes writing* is a bit misleading.

Q: In what way?

A: This kind of writing is "low-stakes" in the sense that the student knows his or her teacher will not be assessing, grading, or correcting it. But such writing can be extremely important to the student who wrote it—a note from a boy to a girl he likes, an apology letter to mom, an agreement between brothers, and so on. These issues often matter greatly to the writer.

Q: Is all this scribbling and jotting and typing really writing?

A: Absolutely. Most teachers I talked to agree with me. Kate Kuonen, a junior high teacher, put it like this: "Clearly informal writing is writing. It satisfies all the components (meaning, audience, perspective, tone), so it's silly to see it otherwise."

Q: So what is your bumper sticker for greenbelt writing?

A (groan)**:** Yo, didn't you read Chapter 1? I'm not a bumper sticker kind of person.

Q: OK, well, what are some important characteristics of such writing?

A: It should be student-centered. Greenbelt writing isn't created to please the teacher or satisfy some assignment—it's for them. It should be fun and playful. That's why I refer to it as low-stakes. And it should have voice. It should sound like a kid wrote it, not like a grown-up brain stuffed into a kid's brain.

Q: What about choice? Does the student always initiate greenbelt writing?

A: Usually, though not always. Teachers are the ones who initiate the Slice of Life Challenge. But kids should have a choice as to whether or not they want to participate. Real choice is huge. It's one of the defining features of greenbelt writing. In gardening, a *volunteer* is a plant that grows on its own rather than being deliberately planted. I want young writers who view themselves as volunteers, not conscripts.

Q (sighing)**:** Yet another metaphor.

A: What can I say? It's what I do.

Q: In a perfect world shouldn't these essential conditions (choice, voice, play, low-stakes, fun) already exist in the writing workshop?

A: Of course! But, for a variety of reasons, they have become rare, or nonexistent. That's why creating a greenbelt is so important.

Q: So, in a way, the writing greenbelt is a compromise.

A (reluctantly)**:** Yes, I suppose so. I'm a realist.

Q: Should teachers have their students do greenbelt writing instead of workshop writing?

A: No. Including both greenbelt writing and writing workshop will allow these two kinds of writing to rub against each other and cross-pollinate.

Q: Huh?

A: Greenbelt writing will inform and enliven the more formal "school writing." But it works the other way around, as well. The skills kids learn in workshop often show up in their greenbelt writing. In fact, that's the acid test—when you see them using these skills/strategies in their independent writing, you know they truly own them.

"Many of my students benefit from informal writing," Conchetta Marucci told me. She teaches eighth grade. "One student who has really flourished tells me often that if I didn't show her that poetry was so free and, at times, ruleless, she would never have started writing so much of it. In turn, I notice the impact that all of that freedom has had on her formal writing. It allows her to easily insert figurative language where it perfectly fits. Before, I doubt she would have even tried to be anything but literal in her formal writing."

Q: Based on the examples in this book, it seems like audience matters a lot with this kind of writing.

A: For sure. Having supportive, sympathetic readers is really important. But not all greenbelt writing is meant to be shared. Sometimes the student chooses to write for him- or herself, taking solitary pleasure in that work.

Q: In the real world greenbelts exist adjacent to, but separate from, developed communities. This leads me to wonder: what role do teachers have in encouraging students' greenbelt writing?

A: Well, for one thing, the teacher can sanction it. Sometimes it's enough simply to bear witness. "I've noticed a lot of you doing some great writing on your own, or with a buddy . . ."

Also, it's important to model the informal writing we do ourselves: "Every year my wife and I have a Leaf Free or Die party—to get folks to help me rake all the leaves on our lawn. Last night I started making a list of all the people I want to invite." When teachers mention our own low-stakes writing, and demonstrate how we do it in our own lives, it becomes real.

Q: How should teachers confer with students on their informal writing? Or should we even try?

A: It depends on what you mean by *confer*. I think it would look different from a typical writing conference.

Q: Different how?

A: Take a look at the graph in Figure 12.1. The two factors here are the teacher's input and the teacher's interest. In a typical conference, the expectation is that the teacher will provide *high interest* in the student's writing, and *high input*, as well. Kids expect the teacher to weigh in, suggest a strategy/craft move, or give a challenge.

The graph in Figure 12.2 shows how teachers might respond to students' greenbelt writing. We should still communicate that we're very interested in what the student is working on. But our input should be low.

Q: So, just back off? Don't correct?

A (nodding)**:** Cut 'em loose. Let 'em write. And make sure the student knows that he or she is the one who's driving the bus.

Q: Don't grade it?

A: God, no!

Q (pause)**:** That doesn't feel like teaching.

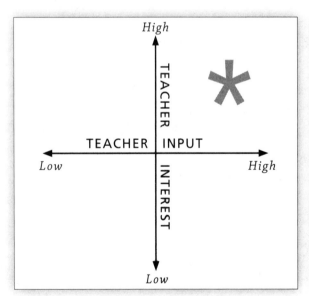

Figure 12.1: Conferring in Writing Workshop

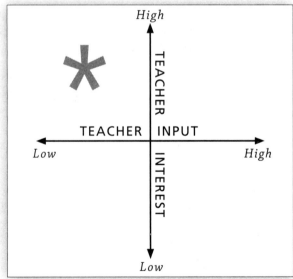

Figure 12.2: Responding to Informal/ Greenbelt Writing

A: A writing greenbelt is a space where students can go to play. It gives them time, place, and opportunity to teach themselves to write by actually writing about what interests them in the way they want to write about it. (Smile) What a concept! There is another kind of feedback we can give students when they show us this writing. As I wrote earlier, many teachers told me that their students don't perceive this as writing.

Q: Really?

A: Apparently so. The kids figure if it's not part of a genre study or unit of study, well, it can't be "real" writing. It's like believing that you can't really exercise unless you go to your gym. Which, of course, is ridiculous. You can get a great workout, and burn beaucoup calories, by working in the garden, raking leaves, or washing windows.

So when kids write informally, it's important that we give them a clear message: what you're doing *is* writing. Don't assume that they know this, because they may not. You've got to tell them explicitly.

Q: Should teachers give out praise for this kind of writing?

A: Sure, if it's genuine praise. And that can be tricky. Some teachers have confided to me that it isn't always easy for them to praise such writing.

"I do think informal writing can build stamina, especially the long fiction stories," says Naomi Marotta, a fourth-grade teacher. "My kids are usually very enthusiastic for me to read these pieces. But I have to say, as a teacher who spends time teaching them how to use paragraphs, punctuation, and so on, I find it difficult to get through these pieces with a smile on my face."

I appreciated her candid response. One other thing: it really helps to understand what the kid is trying to accomplish in the writing because that will guide us to the best way to celebrate it. If a boy is writing a comic for his preschool-age brother, you might say: "Your brother will *love* that! Don't forget to take it home so he can read it, or you can read it to him." Or if two girls are working on a story that now stretches for twenty-two pages, you could say: "Wow, that's amazing—I bet you've never written anything so long!"

Don't be surprised if your kids bite off more than they can chew with their greenbelt writing. But even when they fall short, as they certainly will, you should still celebrate the effort. It's the attempt that matters.

Q: Where should kids do this kind of writing? In school or out?

A: Both. Ideally, a teacher will create a space (or spaces) for greenbelt writing during the school day. Putting it on the class schedule is a way to show students that we value it. But much of the greenbelt writing will happen outside class, at home.

One important measure of how successful we are teaching writing is how much writing kids do at home. (The same thing is true for reading, by the way.) Our students know how to write, but do they choose to write at home? When they write at home they're giving us important information. They're letting us know that writing has become part of who they are.

Q: What are some other ways we can show kids that we value their greenbelt writing?

A: If you see some strong writing, use it as model in a minilesson: "Joseph and Jared did a great job creating a scary mood at the beginning of the horror story they're working on. Listen to the first paragraph." By doing so, you're letting kids see that this kind of writing has legitimate value, a place in the world.

Q: What do you see as the main benefits of greenbelt writing? You've already mentioned stamina and engagement. And you talked about its potential impact on the reluctant writer.

A: In my survey I asked teachers: "What value do you place on this kind of writing?" Many replied: "Students come to see themselves as writers." That's not a trivial thing. That self-identity—*I am a writer*—is everything. That's what we're shooting for.

Q: Anything else? What about pleasure?

A (deadpan)**:** I'm for it.

Q: Really. So you're pro-joy?

A: Absolutely. Look, I realize that when someone else is arguing for rigor and I'm arguing for joy, well, that's a tough argument to win in today's educational climate. But do we really think our students are nothing more than passive automatons that will soak up all our content about essays? It's crucial that they enjoy it, as well. I urge teachers to move fun and joy higher up on their list of priorities. Let's make the writing classroom a joyful place. There you go—that's a bumper sticker I can live with.

Q: Do you see any other benefits to this low-stakes writing you're talking about?

A: One thing I haven't mentioned—this kind of writing can help build community.

"The low-stakes nature of informal writing allows kids to take risks, to find joy and purpose in writing," says Dalila Eckstein, a third-grade teacher. "Once my most reluctant writers build some momentum, we begin to gel as a writing community. I notice that my writers start supporting/encouraging each other more. They advocate for themselves and request time and opportunities to write what they want and to share it."

Dalila adds: "This approach pays dividends when teaching what is required because we build muscles from writing that has a high level of interest and engagement."

Q: Do you see this kind of low-stakes writing as a side dish, or the main course, in a writing curriculum?

A: Depends. Teachers, of course, are notoriously time-crunched. In many schools, writing has found a permanent home in the curriculum in the form of writing workshop, a one-hour block devoted to helping improve student writing. Realistically, writing workshop will probably be the main course.

But many students—more than we might imagine—will find their stride through greenbelt writing. That's where they will (re)discover the passion of writing, the thrill of saying exactly what you want to say and how you want to say it, savoring how it feels when you create every word, comma, exclamation point and can say with proud confidence: "This is what I wrote—and it's all mine."

Q: With all due respect, the idea of setting up a writing greenbelt sounds pretty idealistic in this test-centric, data-driven educational world. Wouldn't you agree?

A: No, I would not. Look, tree-hugging hippies aren't the ones who make green spaces—city planners create them. These folks are not exactly daydreamers. They are unsentimental types, people who have to deal with zoning, tax codes, and right-of-way statutes on a daily basis. But they understand the tangible benefits that green spaces bring to a community. So they carve out an area on the map, set that land aside, and protect it from development.

Something like that needs to happen in school. Curriculum coordinators should create writing greenbelts on the curriculum map. Teachers should be encouraged to create them in the classroom.

. . .

This final chapter is written in a playful style, but it shouldn't be construed as a signal that I'm fooling around because I'm not. I'm dead serious. In Bangkok, Thailand, there's a green space called Bang Krachao. My wife and I spent time there when we visited Bangkok a few years ago. Going to Bang Krachao is disorienting because you have to make an abrupt transition from urban life into near-wilderness. It's hard to realize that you're still in Bangkok when you suddenly find yourself walking past lush jungle, swamps, bike paths (no cars allowed), and wildlife (lizards, tree vipers, and pythons). Bang Krachao is known as "Bangkok's lung" because it provides fresh oxygen for the city. Even if the residents don't visit very often, they know it's there.

A writing greenbelt plays the same important role in the classroom. It opens the window and lets in a wave of fresh air—something that's sorely missing in too many writing classrooms. A writing greenbelt creates an environment where young writers can flourish, have fun, produce both quantity and quality, and discover for themselves the myriad pleasures of writing.

The End

Birthday List
by Joseph

Joseph's List Birthday

1. Lord of the Rings Risk.
2. mario Kart double Dash (vidioe Game).
3. StraBe light.
4. tatoo pens.
5. my Watch Fixed.
6. Zelda four Sword S (came Boy Game)

IN PAREN's HANds ONLY!

December 3   Tuseday

Dear Santa,
I need your help to find the
perfect gift for my mom, my dad,
and Ethan. I also wanted to know
what a house elf is because
some kids in my class were talking
about them.
              Love,
              Eliza

P.S. My Christmas list is on
the way!

There home!

Is this
what they look
like.

Letter to Santa
by Eliza

Exploratory Writing

This kind of informal writing can be used to:

- Activate prior knowledge.

- Generate questions, wonderings, speculations.

- Make a map or web of your topic.

- Collect surprising information, facts, statistics.

- React: What amazes/appalls you about the topic?

- Make a prediction.

- Build a lexicon or glossary of words or terms specific to the subject.

- Draw or sketch.

- Sift, sort, summarize.

- Try a "flashdraft" on the topic.

The Writer's Notebook

RALPH FLETCHER

Writing in a notebook is a way to fuel up. Supreme superior unleaded. And it's free.
—NAOMI SHIHAB NYE, POET

Breathing In

1. What moves you?

2. What do you wonder about?

3. What do you notice?

4. List seed ideas or "triggers."

5. Use small details.

6. Include snatches of talk.

7. Add memories.

8. Use lists and artifacts.

9. Create writing that inspires.

Breathing Out

1. Reread: dig out the crystals.

2. Experiment with wordplay: write off a text, for example.

3. Try out a set piece.

4. Make a place to write badly.

5. Create writing that scrapes the heart.

6. Write about writing.

REFERENCES

Ayres, Ruth, and Stacey Shubitz. 2010. *Day by Day: Refining Writing Workshop Through 180 Days of Reflective Practice*. Portland, ME: Stenhouse.

Bragg, Rick. 2002. "Skeleton Plunges Face-First Back Into the Winter Games." *New York Times*, Feb. 17.

Cambourne, Brian. Toward an educationally relevant theory of literacy learning: Twenty years of inquiry. *The Reading Teacher: a journal of the International Literacy Association* 1995, 49, (3), 182–192.

Cameron, Julia. 1992. *The Artist's Way: A Spiritual Path to Higher Creatvity*. New York: Hall Street Books.

Fletcher, Ralph. 1996a. *Breathing In, Breathing Out: Keeping a Writer's Notebook*. Portsmouth, NH: Heinemann.

———. 1996b. *A Writer's Notebook: Unlocking the Writer Within You*. New York: HarperCollins.

———. 2013. *What a Writer Needs*, 2nd ed. Portsmouth, NH: Heinemann.

———. 2015. *Making Nonfiction from Scratch*. Portland, ME: Stenhouse.

Graves, Donald. 1993. *Primary Voices K–6*. National Council of Teachers of English.

Heard, Georgia, and Jennifer McDonough. 2009. *A Place for Wonder: Reading and Writing Nonfiction in the Primary Grades*. Portland, ME: Stenhouse.

McPhee, John. 1996. *Oranges*. New York: Farrar, Straus.

Newkirk, Thomas, and Penny Kittle. 2013. *Children Want to Write: Donald Graves and the Revolution in Children's Writing*. Portsmouth, NH: Heinemann.

Ray, Katie Wood. 2006. *Study Driven: A Framework for Planning Units of Study in the Writing Workshop*. Portsmouth, NH: Heinemann.

Wolfe, Tom. 2004. *I Am Charlotte Simmons*. New York: Farrar, Straus.

Help writers grow with more resources from Ralph Fletcher

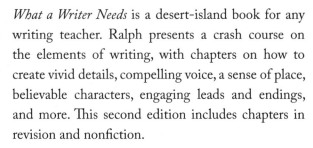

What a Writer Needs is a desert-island book for any writing teacher. Ralph presents a crash course on the elements of writing, with chapters on how to create vivid details, compelling voice, a sense of place, believable characters, engaging leads and endings, and more. This second edition includes chapters in revision and nonfiction.

Grades K–12 • 978-0-325-04666-2

With 24 whiteboard-projectable pieces by Ralph (and online audio files of him reading some of them) as well as writer's notes to share with students, *Mentor Author, Mentor Texts* is not only a collection of mentor texts but also a rare peek for young writers into the author's craft.

Grades 3–8 • 978-0-325-04089-9

Writing Workshop reveals what a potent tool the writing workshop can be for empowering young writers, providing everything a teacher needs to get the writing workshop up and running. In clear language, Ralph and JoAnn explain the simple principles that underlie the writing workshop and explore the major components that make it work.

Grades K–8 • 978-0-325-00362-7